Shifting Paradigms for Men Transformation Through Renewed Vision

COPYRIGHT © 2016 LUVARA PRUDHOMME
WWW.YOURMINDSHIFT.COM
ALL RIGHTS RESERVED.

ISBN 978-0-9908859-2-4

FOREWORD

Shifting Paradigms Series is the good news that answers so many dark questions of life that so often overshadow ones dreams and bankrupts their faith account. This guide is a balance of personal experience, backed by a biblical foundation that seals the power to apply.

Each of us who take on the challenge to use this instructive guiding light of hope to illuminate misguided pathways and increase self-awareness are empowered to shift the platform of our outlook on life. This shining moment could not have presented itself at a greater time than now.

LuVara's universal, personal and Christ-centered experiences afford her the ability to unleash a dramatic outlook on the core of life and the human process that leads to personal inventory. Readers are given a chance to fill in the blank spaces within their own lives. This is what I call "turn the corner of life", where the reader is brought to the well to drink of the author's rich experience but leave with a taste of their own as their pail of reality is drawn from the well of life.

We are thankful for her tenacity to release the God given gift so that others may be blessed as she pushes the margin and raises the bar on life's greater expectations. By allowing God to push and guide her pen to produce the life rays of hope that beams into the lives of others, her work unearths the treasure deep within.

It has been my privilege to interact with LuVara through her efforts to address the issues as is. Through the art of keeping it real, the facts and feelings are attached to real life experiences that echo the silent voice of so many.

Be prepared to find the rich blessing that lies within the rows of each chapter new mercies day by day.

I declare that this book is the springboard that propels your thinking, enriches your life and shifts your paradigm.

Bishop Melvin Brown
Pastor, My Father's House Ministries

Table of Contents

INTRODUCTION........8

CHAPTER 1
Shift My What?........12

CHAPTER 2
What Does My Past Say About Me??........15

CHAPTER 3
What does God say about me?........31

CHAPTER 4
Exposure........56

CHAPTER 5
Who Am I?........68

CHAPTER 6
Learning To Value Myself........79

CHAPTER 7
Breaking Curses........98

CHAPTER 8
Determining Who I Want To Be........106

CHAPTER 9
Living Purposefully..152

CHAPTER 10
Sustaining TheShift..161

SHIFTING PARADIGMS FOR MEN
INTRODUCTION

I believe, Dear Student, that it is no coincidence that you picked up this book. It was written just for you. There is something that is said here or a shared experience that will allow you to receive the healing and deliverance that you need to live a full and whole life. God ordained it this way. This book is a pit stop on the road to your destination; you can be fed, refreshed, refueled, and strengthened for the rest of your journey.

As you go through each chapter it's imperative that you are open and honest and really take time to work through each area that's covered and continually assess every area of your life. There may be things that you are uncomfortable with and don't want to think about or share with others but healing and deliverance starts with exposure.

I'm learning this even more as I write this book. I am a talker, I love talking but I am not a sharer; I do not share my life or experiences with others. I have a therapist for that. You won't find me in the grocery store talking to a stranger about anything personal. Although when I'm out and about many strangers talk to me about their personal lives. I can have a conversation with someone for hours and they will leave not knowing any more about me than when the conversation began. I, on the other hand, will know their whole life story.

Maybe you're wondering why I'm telling you this. I first started writing this book in 2012. Bishop Melvin Brown of My Father's House Ministries in Charleston, South Carolina asked me to put something together for a women's mission. The church had started ministering in a low income apartment complex for women and children. I greatly admire and respect Bishop Brown and was excited that he'd asked me so

I immediately started working on Shifting Paradigms. I was doing pretty good, had an outline and the first chapter completed when news came that one of my favorite uncles had died. I was very sad. After coming back from attending his funeral in Louisiana I didn't feel like writing anymore. When you write you're kind of in your own head and I needed a break from thinking. About 6 months later one of my great aunts died. I had great respect for my aunt and had actually followed in her footsteps by getting a master's degree in Education and planning to get my Ph.D. in Education also.

Experiencing so much loss really put me off my writing game I really didn't want to continue the book because I just didn't feel like writing anymore. But God had you in mind. He knew that at this point in your life you would need the words that He inspired me to write. He knew they would be relevant and life changing for you. So although it took me over a year to start writing again, it's all in God's perfect timing because the day that this book hits your hand is the day that your life will begin to change.

When I started to write again God spoke to me and said "it's time for the rest of the story". It brought to mind Paul Harvey back in the day on the radio when he would take you a little deeper into a news story and his tagline was "and now the rest of the story". I started having visions of speaking before crowds of women, which really didn't bother me but what bothered me is that I was telling them things that I would only tell my therapist. Every time I would envision myself speaking to the crowd I would be letting all of my secrets out of the bag. I was exposing myself. I talked to God about this because I felt I could be effective without having to share my life so openly with others. I have preached and taught for years but I haven't had to tell all of my business. From time to time the Holy Spirit would move me to share with someone and I would give them a piece of my testimony and that was okay but I was not okay with this tell all.

I really tried to convince God that it wasn't necessary for me to share personal things to be effective, I stopped having the visions so I felt maybe I'd made headway. Plus, I hadn't been invited to any speaking engagements anyway so I decided that I'd cross that bridge when I got to it. Needless to say that was not God's plan. He wanted me to tell the rest of the story here in this book. Every chapter that has anything about my personal life in it was written after I thought I had completed the book. During my review, I began to add more to some of the chapters and the more I wrote the more I opened my own life. God said to me, "How can you relate to them if they don't know your story?" How will they know that you've sat where they sit, in grave clothes, surrounded by ashes, wanting to lie down and give up, considering suicide, even contemplating homicide, feeling so down and so low that it took all of your strength just to lift up your head. He reminded me that I was trying to be strong, trying to be everything for everybody but neglecting myself. I looked like I had it all together but I was really empty, lonely and dissatisfied. I didn't know how I would make it but I decided to live for Him and I made it. He also said, "You are an overcomer, you broke through the pain, the depression and the disappointments and you live victoriously."

I remembered that God did not save, deliver or heal me just for me and what was the point of going through all of that hell if I wasn't going to use it to help someone else avoid it or come through it. I did not come to this easily and I wasn't as resigned as I may sound; I was still kicking and screaming. I didn't tell my entire life story but I'm glad that I did share some things because there is healing in sharing. There were still areas in my life where I needed full deliverance and as I began to write about and think about them I was able to basically "write out" the pain and hurt.

God is so amazing and awesome. He knows just what we need and how we need it. He knew that I needed more deliverance in areas that I never focus on and He knew that you needed to know that you are not alone and that there is light at the end of the tunnel. I pray that as you read this book and go through the lessons that you will begin to see your life change in a miraculous way, that you will be transformed by the renewing of your mind and allow your paradigm to shift.

To get the most out of this book I recommend that you do it in a group or at least with one other person. Hearing others' experiences can help you open up and share your own or realize that you're not alone. Being accountable to someone else also keeps you focused and on track. If you are interested in going through the book with a group and having someone facilitate, an instructor guide is available. You will be amazed at how dynamic a group setting can be for growth and change.

Write me and let me know how this revelation and inspiration from God blesses you.

Your Sister In Christ,

LuVara R. Prudhomme

SHIFTING PARADIGMS FOR MEN

CHAPTER I

Shift My What?

I allowed a couple of people whose opinions I greatly value to read and critique the books that I'm writing for this series. Although they understood what the word paradigm meant they felt that I needed to be a little more specific so that my readers would understand what I'm asking them to do. My goal in writing this series is to help you realize that to change your life you must change your thinking, your outlook, your actions and your reactions. I'm not presuming that you're unhappy with your life but everyone has something that is stopping them from living their best life. It could be something from your past or fear of your future. I want to help you face those challenges clearly, boldly and completely.

Shifting Paradigms is the answer that God gave me to help you undertake this huge challenge.

A **paradigm** is a theory or a group of ideas about how something should be done, made, or thought about.

Shifting means to change or to cause (something) to change to a different opinion, belief, etc.

A paradigm shift is an important change that happens when the usual way of thinking about or doing something is replaced by a new and different way.

In this series, our definition of **Shifting Paradigms** is to change your beliefs about the way you think, the things that you do or how you make decisions.

The aim of this series is to encourage you to take a second look or in some cases maybe a first look at yourself and examine everything that affects you and how and why it affects you... home, environment, relationships, and future.

For example, I grew up very superstitious. I'm not sure if it was being from Louisiana that caused that or just growing up in the environment that I grew up in but there were many things that I felt a certain way about and for many years of my life my superstitions governed my life. When I went to the beauty shop to get my hair cut, my beautician had to sweep up all of my hair and put it in a bag so that I could take it with me. I never split poles. If I just happened to be walking with someone and we split a pole I'd go back and go around the pole the same way the person I was walking with went around it. I didn't believe in walking under ladders. I hated black cats because they could just ruin my whole day. Pointing at graveyards was just not done. If someone accidentally swept my foot, I'd almost waste the whole box of salt. There are other things but I'm sure that you have the picture...I was extremely superstitious. When my relationship with Christ began to really grow I began to see that a lot of those superstitions were just ridiculous. My destiny wasn't in the hands of chance but in the hands of a loving, merciful God that had already predestined my life. It was not easy to let go of beliefs that I'd had for my entire childhood and many adult years. Sometimes even now some of them rear their ugly heads and I have to self-talk to remind myself that I no longer allow superstitions to control me. This is what I'm asking you to do. Take a look at those things that control you and determine why they have that kind of control over you. I'm not saying that everything is bad, there are some things that aren't bad they're just not good.

As you go through the series your main focus will need to be on yourself. I know that may be hard for some of you but it's necessary. This course is all about you! The main requirement when you enter the doors of the class is to turn off everything and everyone and give yourself uninterrupted time to just focus on you. Also you must be open and honest with yourself even if it hurts, or brings up unwanted feelings or emotions. The classroom is your sanctuary there is no right or wrong answer and there is no judgement. Think of it as a time for you to come and get therapy from a small group of people that will also need therapy from you. It's an opportunity to share your hurts, disappointments, successes and dreams with others that are eager to encourage, embrace, and celebrate with you.

At first opening up and being honest with yourself and others around you will be challenging, you may even get upset and not want to participate. You won't be alone in feeling that... no one wants to be vulnerable, no one wants to expose themselves and let others know their pain and suffering but I'm challenging you to get over it! These next 16 weeks are not about what anyone else thinks or feels about you, your past, your mistakes, your decisions, and your dreams; it's about what you think. It's about what you need to be whole, to be healed, to be delivered and to be set on a path of purpose towards your great destiny.

Yes, it will be challenging! It will be hard! It will be uncomfortable! But it will be for your good and ultimately for God's glory!

I challenge you to focus on shifting your paradigm for the next 16 weeks of this class and watch how your life changes!

I believe in you! You got this!

SHIFTING PARADIGMS FOR MEN

CHAPTER 2

What Does My Past Say About Me??

Everything that we have done in our past has shaped our present and will shape our future. Many people can't change their lives presently because they have not dealt with those issues in the past that affect every decision that they make and is the reason they are where they are now. As humans we are not always able to handle the difficulties that we experience so at every stage of our lives we automatically implement coping mechanisms. In childhood, escapism and repression are coping mechanisms that many of us learn or are taught. Escapism is the tendency to escape from daily reality or routine by indulging in daydreaming, fantasy, or entertainment. If we are living in an abusive environment, to cope, we mentally escape that environment and build a better, safer place in our minds.

When we're children we aren't able to escape physically, as a matter of fact the idea of escaping or running away can be more traumatizing than dealing with the reality of the abuse. If we are experiencing abuse or see a loved one being abused, instead of feeling powerless and helpless we may escape to our dream world where everything is calm and peaceful. Repression goes hand in hand with escapism. **Repression** is the **unconscious** exclusion of painful impulses, desires, or fears from the conscious mind. When we're young we repress our feelings. There are many reasons we repress them; if the abuser still lives in the home with us we are still seeking their love and approval so we have to "forget" the pain that they've caused us. We hide the pain and fear in our subconscious mind for as long as we can or put it somewhere safe in our dream world when we escape. Unfortunately our minds cannot hide things forever and eventually that pain and those fears begin to resurface. We then employ another coping mechanism, suppression. **Suppression** is the **conscious** exclusion of unacceptable desires, thoughts, or memories from the mind; unlike repression when we unconsciously did it (unknowingly, not realizing that we were doing it) we are now purposely doing it.

Let's examine repression and suppression more in detail. When I was growing up my mom had a couple of sayings: don't cry over spilled milk, a woman's gotta do what a woman's gotta do, and one monkey don't stop no show. I don't think she realized how much of an impact those words would make in my life. I latched on to them and they became my mantra for life as a matter of fact many times they propelled me to keep going when situations were at their worst. They also caused me to repress and suppress a lot of things. I didn't consciously or knowingly exclude painful or hurtful things from my mind I had conditioned myself to let my mantras take over and I would focus less on the pain and hurt and more on getting beyond it. I would say to myself, don't cry over spilled milk, find a way to wipe it up. My rationale was if I was crying I wasn't thinking, if I wasn't thinking I couldn't find a way out of the situation. I was always looking for solutions to keep me moving and I would tuck the situation in a corner in my mind to deal with later. I never saw this as avoidance because I would deal with the situation but I didn't deal with the impact of the situation. I never cried about or allowed myself to feel hurt over it, before we started using the phrase, keep it moving, I was keeping it moving.

I would pull out "a woman's gotta do what a woman's gotta do" normally when I had been disappointed or someone had let me down, usually a man; my first husband to be exact. He always called me superwoman but I wasn't trying to be superwoman I was trying to survive. My first husband didn't do what I wanted him to do, needed him to do, or thought he should do fast enough for me. When we were together I felt like I had to take care of everything. We were living two completely different lives in the same house; he was living a life of leisure and I was always working, always pregnant and always miserable. I would vent from time to time but he didn't really seem to hear me so I would just encourage myself doing "what a woman's gotta do" and keep everything moving forward, after all I had a daughter to take care of and I didn't want her to suffer. Even when I divorced him I was "doing what a woman's got to do" I didn't cry about it nor did I allow myself to feel hurt over it, you know what I did, I kept it moving.

My favorite saying was "One monkey don't stop no show" because instead of muttering this to myself and gaining personal strength and courage from it like I did with "don't cry over spilled milk" and "a woman's gotta do what a woman's gotta do" I would actually yell this to whoever was not on board with my plans, wasn't a team player, didn't hold up their end of the bargain or were just absent. I would say, "please believe one monkey don't stop no show." I would say it in such a way that they understood that they were the monkey that I was talking about and I didn't need them for anything. I would say it with lots of attitude and bravado and then walk away like they were invisible to me. My goal was to always stay strong because you know only the strong survive. I didn't realize that my approach was both repressive and suppressive. I never thought about it. My goal was to get on the other side of problems and not let them destroy me.

I am the oldest of 7 children. My mother was a single parent, even when she was married, she was a single parent. There was never anyone to help her in child rearing. My siblings and I are nine years apart; so imagine that, 7 children in 9 years. My mom grew up very different from the way that we grew up. She grew up with an abundance of everything. My great grandmother was wealthy and provided for everybody. All of my family lived together, right next to each other on farmland that we owned. My great grandparents, grandfather, aunts, uncles, and cousins all lived there. It was great because for meals you had so many options, there was a lot of safety and freedom and all of my cousins to play with.

The summer before my 9th grade year my mother and siblings moved to another city. I did not want to go so my mother allowed me to finish my 9th grade year in our small town. When school ended my mother came the same day to pick me up. I was devastated. I was not ready for a move and especially not ready to leave all of my friends and family to move to a much larger city. On top of all of that I think my mom had found the smallest house in the city for 8 people. We had to share bedrooms and there was no privacy at all. This was really the first time that my mom was on her own without the support of my great grandmother and it was quite obvious that she was trying her best to make it work. As a result I began to take on more responsibility for helping our family succeed. This was when my life changed because I felt that I had to be strong for my siblings and for my mom. I knew that she was doing all that she knew how to do to make things better for us and the things that she couldn't fix, she loved us through. Love was like a Band-Aid for us.

During these years, being strong was the most important thing to me. My definition of strength was: no crying, no letting them see you sweat, not really asking for help, no giving up, and no backing down. I have been strong my entire life. If you really think about it people always tell you to be strong and not to cry. Being strong has caused many people heart attacks, strokes and aneurysms and put many in an early grave. We were not created to be an island; to take everything on ourselves and try to handle everything by ourselves.

For years, I zipped through life happily with my strength and mantras in place overcoming issue after issue; miscarriage after miscarriage, failed marriage, single parenting, death, disappointments, career setbacks, credit set- backs, money issues, and everything in between. In 2000, I decided to finally submit to the call on my life and really began to seek God through prayer. As I began to pray and talk to God, He began to remind me of very old issues; things that had happened when I was very young.

My father has never been in my life. I remember him coming by to see me once when I was very young, he took a splinter out of my finger and sang me to sleep. I talked to him on the phone a couple of times and he told me that the reason he didn't come around is because I had a stepfather and he didn't want to cause problems. After I turned 18 years old and had gone to the Air Force, I came home on leave and went to my father's house. I asked the child that came to the door to get his mother. My mom taught me to respect people so I didn't want to just show up demanding to see her husband. She came to the door and I called her by name and asked if I could see my father. She told me that I didn't have a father there, only her husband lived there. I again called her by name and said please don't play with me and asked again to see my father. She finally reluctantly went to get her husband.

See I grew up in the very small town of Natchitoches Louisiana if you've heard of it it's only because Steel Magnolias was filmed there and Oprah visited there once. We also are famous for our Christmas festival and parade and meat pies. It's so small that everybody knows everybody or at least they know some of your kin. When my cousins and I would go out joy riding and clowning my great grandmother would know everywhere we'd been before we got back home. So it was no secret to anyone that this man was my father and even less of a secret since I looked just like him.

When she came back to the door with her husband I said, "Hi Richard I just came by to visit, I'm an adult now and don't need anything from you, I just want to have a relationship with you." I figured now that a stepfather was no longer an issue, he and I could have a relationship. The man that came to the door with a face like mine, looked at me with eyes that are just like mine and from a mouth shaped exactly like mine said to me "you have the wrong house, I'm not who you're looking for, I'm not your daddy." I always knew exactly where my father lived and had visited a family friend across the street and had gone to a beauty shop around the corner for years. I was really taken aback and honestly I must have kind of blacked out for a minute (I realized later in life that when I'm about to do something that will be very traumatic for other people and land me in jail or worse, it's almost like God allows me to black out for a few minutes to give my brain time to fall back into place) because the next thing I remember was my sister, who was waiting in the car, pulling me off the steps, into the yard and back into the car. This time and when I was very young are the only two times that I ever saw my father. I have not seen him again since that day 26 years ago.

For many years everything I did was done in the face of my father, he didn't know, could care less and wasn't even looking but I was always trying to prove to him that his rejection of me didn't stop me from succeeding one bit. In time my whole attitude towards him was "one monkey don't stop no show" and I got over it because I realized that I was performing for an empty audience and there's no satisfaction in that. Through the years I didn't even think about my father much so I was very surprised when during my conversation with God about my ministry, He brought up my father. Actually I wasn't just surprised I was upset. "Why would you remind me of that", I asked, "what does that have to do with my ministry?" God said "that hurt you", I said "no, I wasn't hurt I was just disappointed but that's okay because he missed out, plus I didn't need him anyway." God insisted that I was hurt and I just as vehemently denied being hurt. I could accept being everything but hurt: disappointed, disillusioned, let down, cursed with bad luck; anything but hurt. Because God is God and knows me better than I know myself, He began to win the battle. The last time He told me that I was hurt, I began to cry. I never cried unless I watched really sad movies, *King Kong, Beaches* and *The Notebook*, get me everytime.

The truth is, I didn't cry well and hearing myself cry was always strange. Whenever I'd begin to cry I would start talking to myself saying, "No Reneé you got this, don't cry about this, it's okay" I would then begin to laugh and stop crying. That was normally how crying happened for me. I would think about how silly it is to cry over what I considered spilled milk and I would begin to laugh, dry my eyes, blow my nose and get back to something productive. That did not work this time, see I didn't realize that I was actually beginning to be delivered and this was just the first night. I didn't know that I had 29 more nights to go. 29 more nights of having God shuffle through my mind and dig up all of the hurts and pain from the past. 29 more nights of sobbing uncontrollably because the little girl had started repressing and suppressing very early. I actually had to deal with every single thing that I had pushed aside; that my mantras had seen me through but I had not dealt with. There were things that I had repressed for so long that I thought God may have been showing me someone else's memories. I didn't realize that so many things had hurt me. I would cry so hard that I would be gasping for air and my body would be shaking. I relived every moment of pain. I could see the faces or the situations so clearly that it felt like it was happening all over again. There were countless things that I relived during my deliverance sessions, too many things to name but some of the events were life changing and I tried never to even think about the loss and pain associated with them. God would not let me hide any longer from the past and the pain of the past. Another area that was just as painful for me to deal with as dealing with my father's rejection was the failure of my first marriage.

I met my first husband in 1985. I was 17 years old and a senior in high school. He was 18 and a freshman in college. I met him at a basketball game, actually I had just quit the girl's team and didn't want to stay around to watch the boys play. I walked out of the gym and through the quadrangle and heard someone call my name. When I turned to see who called me I looked into the face of a tall, dark, stranger. He introduced himself and pretended that he and I had met, he knew the name of the private school that I'd attended and even knew where I lived but I knew I had never met him because I remember faces. He was adamant that we'd met before and even began to tell me personal things about myself. I started to feel leery and began to walk away. Later, he told me that he was just testing my character. We had never met but he was sitting at the game with a guy that lived down the street from me and when he saw me leave the gym he asked the guy about me. He said if I had agreed that we'd met he would have walked away. We began a courtship that had everybody's tongue wagging. He had graduated from that high school the year before but never dated anybody. I was technically the "new girl" because I only went there my senior year and there were several girls still there that really liked him and they were jealous that I'd snagged him.

He was my first love. I had dated other guys but it was nothing like this; I was on cloud 9. He would sing to me, we'd go places together, dance under the stars, and plan our future. He would park at my house and walk to the school to pick me up. I loved walking to and from school. I had begged my mother the entire summer to let me attend that school so I could walk. The soundtrack of our relationship was smooth, mellow, and full of love; Sade, Stevie Wonder, Luther Vandross and lite rock were our stations. I knew that he was the man that I wanted to spend the rest of my life with.

When we got married in 1988, I was overjoyed. I couldn't believe that finally I would get to spend every day and night with my best friend, my confidant and the love of my life. Every day was a great day, but my favorite day was Saturday. We would wake up Saturday mornings and lie in bed talking about our hopes and dreams and making plans for our future. Afterwards we'd make love and then he'd get up to cook brunch for us; I treasured that time together more than any other time. I could not imagine having a life without him, we were one, inseparable, we were extensions of each other. In my mind hurting him would be like hurting myself. So the day that our marriage ended I felt like someone had sliced me in two and cut out my heart.

Years later when I looked back on all of the mistakes that we made and all of the misunderstandings that we had I realized that our major problem was lack of good role models and a support system. We both knew what we didn't want in a marriage by looking at our parents and the marriages that they had but we didn't know what we did want in a marriage or what we needed to have a successful marriage. I had only seen one successful marriage and that was my great uncle and his wife and they were very old. I didn't feel like they could relate to me and what I was going through. Our expectations were unrealistic. We had strange ideas about what each person's role was in the relationship. I didn't understand his role because I'd never had a male play a role in my life other than as a brother but I burdened him with the roles of father, husband, lover, best friend, provider, protector, and leader. I expected him to be everything and give me everything that I had missed out on. He tried but failed because he could not be everything to me and he could not give me what I needed from my father. He did not know how to articulate that to me, he was only 20 years old.

To make matters worse, we experienced more loss and pain in the first two years of our marriage than most people experience in a lifetime. We had a premature daughter that stayed in the hospital for three months, followed by an abortion after being told there was a chance that I'd die trying to give birth, followed by a couple of miscarriages and stillbirth of twins. This continual loss forced us to make a decision to not only tie but burn my tubes when I was only 21 years old. There was no one to help us navigate through the pain and fear so we went to opposite corners and licked our wounds. What should have brought us closer together actually just drove us further apart because we didn't know how to communicate our hurt and confusion to each other without anger and blame. We were protecting ourselves from each other when we should have been embracing each other. Coupled with all of this loss we were losing other things too: trust, respect and friendship.

As things began to go from bad to worse and the relationship began to crumble my mantras came to my rescue and held me together. I did not cry over any part of that "spilled" relationship, I refused to allow a "monkey" to stop me from succeeding and I was focused on doing "what I had to do."

When asked about my marriage I was very cavalier about it, I would say that I was very disappointed in how things had worked out when the truth was I was devastated; no one knew how empty and broken I felt. You couldn't look at my life and tell that I was walking around with a big hole where my heart had been. I got up every day and did what a woman's gotta do: went to work, took care of our daughter, met and hung out with new people and had a very active social life. I was the life of the party. I partied like a rock star. No one knew that my smile and party girl attitude was just a lie.

By the time God began to deliver me I had basically been living a lie for 5 long years. When God began to walk me back through the marriage I tried to detach myself from what I was seeing. I tried using my familiar line with God about how disappointed I was but who was I fooling? Surely not an omniscient God. I came to the realization that I had a lot of blame, hurt and anger about the failure of my marriage. My heart was broken and I had never dealt with the loss of not only a husband but a partner and best friend as well. I had been living with the pain and brokenness for over 10 years. I was also very disappointed. I was disappointed in everyone: my ex-husband, myself, our families, friends, co-workers and every person that watched our lives fall apart and did or said nothing. As God began to take me through it all I was finally able to see the truth and for the first time ever I forgave my ex and myself and released that hurt.

What hurt are you still holding and pretending not to have? Men repress and suppress a lot more than women. Many times men can't show weakness, or sensitivity because a man is not a man unless he is considered strong by everyone in his life. That's the narrow, biased thinking that keep many men in bondage and full of hurt, brokenness, and rage. I understand never letting them see you sweat. That's how I lived my life for many years too. It took God breaking me down and forcing me to deal with issues that had eaten away at my life and my character for me to actually get my life back. I'm glad that I submitted to it because I've heard many testimonies of pastors that were laid flat on their backs or close to death before they got it.

Another thing that God showed me was all of the things and people that I'd used to medicate myself. People that I'd hurt and damaged to help me get over the hump; particularly men. I became cold and heartless; my heart was gone so it was easy. No one knew how hard and callous I'd become. I mastered not showing my emotions and easily lured unsuspecting men into my web. I was like a black widow. The female Black Widow is considered the most venomous spider in North America. Her venom is 15 times as toxic as the venom of the prairie rattlesnake and on occasion, the Black Widow will kill and eat the male after they mate. I was poisoning every man that I came into contact with. They didn't realize it because I was a lot of fun and easy to be around. I wasn't clingy, didn't nag, nor did I put any demands on them and they ate up every bit of it. As they drew closer and closer to me I moved further and further from them. I distanced myself from any real feelings and eventually I would end the relationship for one thing or another. I was like a plague infecting one good man after another. I never cared about what they felt until God showed me all of the damage that I did. My heart bled for them and I felt sorrier than I'd ever felt in my life.

Many times men run through women without stopping to think about the damage that they are causing. When a man gets hurt he doesn't admit it many times not even to himself. Some men don't even stop and evaluate what happened or deal with the emotions involved, they just keep going. That's how I was. I just kept medicating my pain. My motto was work hard and play hard. I may not have worked very hard but I definitely played hard. I partied all of the time. I went to happy hour a couple of times a week and out to the club three times a week. The base had all-nighters, where the club stayed open until 5:00 in the morning. That was a big thing back then because most clubs closed at 2:00. I was at every all-nighter; drinking and smoking. I drank like a fish. When I was stationed in Korea they opened a new club across the street from the dorms that I lived in. It was open for 24 hours for the first couple of nights. I spent the night in the club, asleep at the bar. We would take coolers to the bowling alley and get drunk while we bowled.

I would be so drunk that I would pass out and wake up and not even know where I was or how I got there. I never thought about the effects of alcohol while I was drinking I was just glad that it made me feel kind of numb and kept undesirable thoughts at bay. I was able to escape the reality of my life for a little while.

What medication are you using for your pain? What helps you escape the reality of your broken heart and broken dreams? What runs through your mind when you are all alone and the truth stares you in the face? What makes you cry in your beer? I am always amazed at the confessions I hear from some of my guy friends after a couple of glasses too many. There are always past regrets many times involving a woman; regretful actions and words that they have bottled up for years, never acknowledging their true feelings to the person that they have the feelings for. Unlike women who will open themselves up to hurt and rejection, many times men will not do that. They will just allow things to slip through their fingers and live with regret for a lifetime. Even if a man has moved on to someone else and has built a great life, that regret and pain still hangs heavy in his heart. Is this your story? Are you walking around with broken fragments where your heart is supposed to be? Does the past overshadow your present? Will you be made whole? Just like God healed and delivered me, He can deliver you.

Only God knows exactly where your pain lies and what you need to live a whole life.

Going through deliverance was very hard but it was also very miraculous. I got up every day and went to work, ran errands, cooked dinner, basically did everything that I had to do and then afterwards I would go into my prayer closet and deal with more pain than one person should have to live through. The miracle was that I didn't carry it. I woke up the next day refreshed and ready for the day. You would think I would feel sad, hurt or overwhelmed the next day but I didn't. I was being delivered, healed and washed. After the 30 days I felt lighter and free. I had not only been delivered of the past hurt and pains but I'd also been delivered from using the coping mechanisms that had helped me to mask and hide the hurt for so long. I didn't feel a need to be strong anymore because there's no strength in suffering needlessly, I didn't need my mantras anymore even if I happened to use one of them it didn't mean the same thing for me anymore. Since that deliverance session, I've learned how to experience the hurt and pain that inevitably is a part of life, not run away from it. I still don't cry often but when I feel the need to I give in to that need. It still sounds strange to me but I allow myself to wallow in it a little bit, tears heal and cleanse. One of my friends said that having a really good cry ever so often actually makes your skin look better. I'm not sure about that because my face looks red and swollen but I do know that releasing my hurts and pain to a caring God that knows how to heal broken lives and broken hearts gives me a lot of peace and helps me make it through one more day.

Another thing that healing and deliverance helped me to do was to forgive everyone that hurt me, let me down or disappointed me; including my father and first husband. I haven't seen my father or even talked to him since the day he rejected me there has been no opportunity for that yet but in my heart I have forgiven him. The forgiveness that I gave him helped my heart to heal and the hurt is gone away. The same with my first husband we had to be in each other's lives for our daughter's sake but there is no anger and bitterness. We are actually friends now. While I sit here recounting the story to you, I don't feel sad, angry or even disappointed in my father or anyone else. I let all of that go during my deliverance.

The truth is all of us have things that we have repressed and suppressed but eventually we will all have to deal with those deeply buried issues. If we don't deal with them healthily and effectively our past will determine and affect our future. To compensate we began to employ many coping mechanisms that tear down the fabric of our lives; our thinking, self-image, decision making and our quality of life are all impaired. Remember that coping actions are usually symptoms of deeper problems. The best approach is to discover the deeper cause and address this, which will hopefully then result in the coping mechanism disappearing.

Let's identify coping mechanisms [1]:

- Acting out: not coping – giving in to the pressure to misbehave.
- Adaptation: The human ability to adapt.
- Aim inhibition: lowering sights to what seems more achievable.
- Altruism: Helping others to help self.
- Attack: trying to beat down that which is threatening you.
- Avoidance: mentally or physically avoiding something that causes distress.
- Compartmentalization: separating conflicting thoughts into separated compartments.
- Compensation: making up for a weakness in one area by gaining strength in another.
- Conversion: subconscious conversion of stress into physical symptoms.
- Crying: Tears of release and seeking comfort.
- Denial: refusing to acknowledge that an event has occurred.
- Displacement: shifting of intended action to a safer target.
- Dissociation: separating oneself from parts of your life.
- Emotionality: Outbursts and extreme emotion.
- Fantasy: escaping reality into a world of possibility.
- Help-rejecting complaining: Ask for help then reject it. Idealization: playing up the good points and ignoring limitations of things desired.
- Identification: copying others to take on their characteristics.
- Intellectualization: avoiding emotion by focusing on facts and logic.

- Introjection: Bringing things from the outer world into the inner world.
- Passive aggression: avoiding refusal by passive avoidance.
- Performing rituals: Patterns that delay.
- Post-traumatic growth: Using the energy of trauma for good.
- Projection: seeing your own unwanted feelings in other people.
- Provocation: Get others to act so you can retaliate.
- Rationalization: creating logical reasons for bad behavior.
- Reaction Formation: avoiding something by taking a polar opposite position.
- Regression: returning to a child state to avoid problems.
- Self-harming: physically damaging the body.
- Somatization: psychological problems turned into physical symptoms.
- Substitution: Replacing one thing with another.
- Symbolization: turning unwanted thoughts into metaphoric symbols.
- Trivializing: Making small what is really something big.
- Undoing: actions that psychologically 'undo' wrongdoings for the wrongdoer.

Instead of putting any of the coping mechanisms that we've discussed into place there are a number of approaches that we can take to cope in a positive way with problems, including:

- ***Immediate problem-solving:*** Seeking to fix the problem that is the immediate cause of our difficulty.
- ***Root-cause solving:*** Seeking to fix the underlying cause so that the problem will never recur.

- **Benefit-finding:** Looking for the good things amongst the bad.

- **Spiritual growth:** Finding ways of turning the problem into a way to grow spiritually or emotionally.

CHAPTER 3

What does God say about me?

The lie that everyone easily believes and many times is perpetuated in church is that we can be good enough or do good enough to gain God's love. The truth is that God loves everything that He created and the other truth is we can never be good enough or do enough for God to love us anymore than He already does. You can never be good enough, meaning the excuses that you use for putting off a relationship with God (waiting until you get yourself together or waiting until you stop doing wrong) are useless; you will never get there because it is only through God's grace and mercy and the atonement of our sin through Christ that we are even able to stand before God. The song, Jesus Paid It All, basically sums this up. He paid the ultimate sacrifice because frankly nothing we could have done or can do could pay it. So now that we got that out of the way and you realize that God is not interested in your excuses, let's find out what He is interested in.

The first thing that you must get into your head, wrap yourself in, and understand is that you are not a mystery to God; nothing that you are doing is hidden to Him, nothing that you are thinking is hidden to Him, nothing that you are feeling is hidden to Him, nothing that you are going through is hidden to Him…He knows every single thing there is to know about Y O U. Psalms 139:1-18 sums this up beautifully, this is the NIV version but you can go and read it for yourself:

> 1 You have searched me, LORD, and you know me.
>
> 2 You know when I sit and when I rise; you perceive my thoughts from afar.

3. You discern my going out and my lying down; you are familiar with all my ways.

4. Before a word is on my tongue you, LORD, know it completely.

5. You hem me in behind and before, and you lay your hand upon me.

6. Such knowledge is too wonderful for me, too lofty for me to attain.

7. Where can I go from your Spirit? Where can I flee from your presence?

8. If I go up to the heavens, you are there; if I make my bed in the depths, you are there.

9. If I rise on the wings of the dawn, if I settle on the far side of the sea,

10. even there your hand will guide me, your right hand will hold me fast.

11. If I say, Surely the darkness will hide me and the light become night around me,

12. even the darkness will not be dark to you; the night will shine like the day, for darkness is as light to you.

13. For you created my inmost being; you knit me together in my mother's womb.

14. I praise you because I am fearfully and wonderfully made; your works are wonderful, I know that full well.

15. My frame was not hidden from you when I was made in the secret place, when I was woven together in the depths of the earth.

16. Your eyes saw my unformed body; all the days ordained for me were written in your book before one of them came to be.

17. How precious to me are your thoughts, God! How vast is the sum of them!

18. Were I to count them, they would outnumber the grains of sand — when I awake, I am still with you.

Isn't this amazing! Take a moment to really let this soak in. Think about what you were doing before you came to this meeting, what you were feeling throughout the day, about all of the thoughts that you had today, the places that you visited today, all of the words that came out of your mouth today. Are you thinking about them? Guess what? God was there. He heard it, He saw it, He felt it. Wow! Anybody want a do-over? I'm sure that everyone raised their hand or felt that they needed a do-over. The beauty in all of this is that it was the same yesterday, last week, last month, last year, 10 years ago, 20 years ago and so on. He has always been there. There is nothing that you have experienced that God was not there to see. I'm sure that the next question that you have is if He was there why did you have to endure it, right? That's a question that's always hard to answer because as humans we apply human logic to every situation; we can only see things in our own context of right and wrong and good and bad. Our vision is very limited; we don't see spans of time we only see the moment we're in right now. When something bad happens to us we can only understand it in relation to where we are and what we feel when it happens. We can't see in time and what the ripple effect of that bad experience may be. We say that nothing good comes out of anything bad but that's not true; a lot of great victories and success stories have been birthed out of the ashes of what seemed to be defeat. I know this is not a comfortable thing to examine but it is necessary because we must understand that God has a plan for our lives and sometimes pain and suffering is a part of that plan. I understand that it is hard to feel like someone can love you and allow you to experience pain and suffering if they are able to stop it. This may be a hard pill to swallow but sometimes your destiny and your destination hinge on your pain and suffering. Many successful people used pain as a springboard. Let's look at Tyler Perry's life and career.

Tyler Perry's inspirational journey from the hard streets of New Orleans to the heights of Hollywood's A-list is the stuff of American legend. Born into poverty and raised in a household scarred by abuse, Tyler fought from a young age to find the strength, faith and perseverance that would later form the foundations of his much-acclaimed plays, films, books and shows. It was a simple piece of advice from Oprah Winfrey that set Tyler's career in motion. Encouraged to keep a diary of his daily thoughts and experiences, he began writing a series of soul-searching letters to himself. The letters, full of pain and in time, forgiveness, became a healing catharsis. His writing inspired a musical, *I Know I've Been Changed,* and in 1992, Tyler gathered his life's savings and set off for Atlanta in hopes of staging it for sold out crowds. He spent all the money but the people never came, and Tyler once again came face to face with the poverty that had plagued his youth. He spent months sleeping in seedy motels and his car but his faith— in God and, in turn, himself — only got stronger. He forged a powerful relationship with the church, and kept writing. In 1998 his perseverance paid off and a promoter booked *I Know I've Been Changed* for a limited run at a local church-turned-theatre. This time, the community came out in droves, and soon the musical moved to Atlanta's prestigious Fox Theatre. Tyler Perry never looked back. And so began an incredible run of 13 plays, over 16 movies, his first book, *Don't Make A Black Woman Take Off Her Earrings: Madea's Uninhibited Commentaries On Life And Love,* which shot to the top of the New York Times nonfiction bestseller list and remained there for eight weeks. It went on to claim Quill Book Awards for both "Humor" and "Book of the Year" (an unheard-of feat for a first-time author). Tyler expanded his reach to television with the TBS series *House of Payne,* the highest-rated first-run syndicated cable show of all time, which went into syndication after only a year. His follow up effort, *Meet the Browns,* was the second highest debut ever on cable — after *House of Payne.*

In late 2012, Perry teamed up with Oprah Winfrey in an exclusive deal to bring scripted programming to her cable network, OWN. The hour-long drama, *The Haves and The Have Nots* and the half hour sitcom, *Love Thy Neighbor,* along with the upcoming *Single Moms Club.* Tyler also starred in the title role in the Rob Cohen- directed *Alex Cross.*

In the fall of 2008, Perry opened his 200,000 square foot Studio in Atlanta, situated on the former Delta Airlines campus of more than 30 acres. The Studio consists of five sound stages, a post-production facility, a

> pond, a back lot, a 400-seat theater, a private screening room, and designated areas for entertaining and hosting events.
>
> He has won numerous awards to include 12 NAACP Image, BET, Black Movie and MTV Awards.[2] In 2011 he was listed on Forbes as the Most Highly Paid Man in Entertainment.

Wow, pretty impressive. Tyler Perry is a powerhouse. Journalists refer to him as the multi-hyphenate because he is an actor, writer, producer and director. I'm sure all of you have watched a play, movie or sitcom by Tyler Perry. Many of the stories that he tell are filled with abuse, and family and relationship issues. You can see traces of the abusive childhood that he talks about throughout his work. You can make the case that Tyler's success would not have come about without the pain that he suffered because he is able to relate to millions of viewers and movie goers throughout the world. The stories that he weave are filled with issues that many people are still trying to survive but through laughter and comedic characters he gives them hope and inspiration. After living through poverty, experiencing abuse and homelessness, Tyler could feel like God didn't love him because if He had He would not have allowed him to go through all of the hurt and pain in the first place but he understands that God had a plan for his life and would use these experiences to bring that plan to fruition. He realizes that his pain was for a reason beyond his own understanding; he has helped countless people throughout the world and also healed in the process. Despite the trials and tribulations that he has endured, Tyler always gives God glory for his fame and success. He knows where his strength lies. He says, **"Happiness for me is totally just being at peace knowing that, everything I'm doing, God is pleased with that. It's complete peace for me."** [3]

I also want to point out that every person in the bible endured trials and tribulation. Everyone went through pain and suffering; no one was exempt, even Christ. Being denied, taunted, beaten and nailed to a cross was ultimate suffering but from the onset He went through trials. When

Christ was tempted in the wilderness it was God, the Holy Spirit that took Christ into the wilderness to be tempted. Look at Matthew 4:1,"Then was Jesus led up of the **Spirit** into the wilderness **to be tempted** of the devil." The tempter didn't even show up until Jesus had fasted forty days and forty nights and was hungry. Jesus was human, he had to be weak to not have eaten for forty days and forty nights and the first thing that the tempter asked Jesus to do was turn stones into bread. Imagine that, you're hungry, you're in the wilderness, so you're all alone, out in the middle of nowhere, and the first person that you see asks you to do something that can actually help your situation; it had to be hard for Jesus to combat the enemy. Go through the bible and you will see many examples of suffering. We may not think of it this way but many of our favorite bible stories actually show humans suffering; Jonah in the belly of a fish, can you imagine that? Job basically losing everything to include his children and then have to deal with sores and boils all over his body, Hannah praying for a child that she had to give up to the church. There are many examples of suffering but so many examples of God turning that suffering into something mind-blowing that not only helped the sufferer but that helped many others. You must understand that God has a plan for your life that may impact millions and many times it will be through your pain and suffering. Don't misunderstand me, God doesn't make bad things happen, human depravity and evil causes that. God loves you! It is always God's intent that our lives be full of purpose, joy and peace.

He tells us in Jeremiah 29:11,

> 11 "For I know the plans I have for you," declares the LORD, "plans to prosper you and not to harm you, plans to give you hope and a future."

God did not create anything without a purpose. Read Genesis. Everything was created with purpose. From the light that's day to the darkness that's night, for signs, seasons, and for days and years; to the sun to rule the day and the moon to rule the night, the grass and the seas, living creatures to fill the waters and the earth, to man to have dominion over everything to woman for man. Nothing is without purpose. The same applies to you. God did not create you without a purpose. You were put here to fulfill some purpose in the earth. Nothing that you have done has derailed God's plan for your life or his expectation that you will carry out your purpose. I need you to understand this. Your life experiences have not cancelled God's plan for your life.

Let's talk about pain. To really understand pain and why we endure pain we have to go back to the beginning... the actual beginning... Genesis. I'm sure you know the story about Adam and Eve in the Garden of Eden, the devil in the form of a serpent deceiving Eve to eat the fruit, she eats the fruit and gives it to Adam to eat and God kicks them out of the garden. Most people only know the synopsis but either forget or overlook the consequences of that disobedience. Let's look at Genesis, chapter 3.

The Fall

> 1. Now the serpent was more crafty than any of the wild animals the LORD God had made. He said to the woman, "Did God really say, 'You must not eat from any tree in the garden'?"
>
> 2. The woman said to the serpent, "We may eat fruit from the trees in the garden, 3 but God did say, 'You must not eat fruit from the tree that is in the middle of the garden, and you must not touch it, or you will die."
>
> 4. "You will not certainly die," the serpent said to the woman.
>
> 5. "For God knows that when you eat from it your eyes will be opened, and you will be like God, knowing good and evil."
>
> 6. When the woman saw that the fruit of the tree was good for food and pleasing to the eye, and also desirable for gaining wisdom, she took some and ate it. She also gave some to her husband, who was with her, and he ate it.
>
> 7. Then the eyes of both of them were opened, and they realized they

were naked; so they sewed fig leaves together and made coverings for themselves.

8. Then the man and his wife heard the sound of the LORD God as he was walking in the garden in the cool of the day, and they hid from the LORD God among the trees of the garden.

9. But the LORD God called to the man, "Where are you?"

10. He answered, "I heard you in the garden, and I was afraid because I was naked; so I hid."

11. And he said, "Who told you that you were naked? Have you eaten from the tree that I commanded you not to eat from?"

12. The man said, "The woman you put here with me—she gave me some fruit from the tree, and I ate it."

13. Then the LORD God said to the woman, "What is this you have done?" The woman said, "The serpent deceived me, and I ate."

14. So the LORD God said to the serpent, "Because you have done this, "Cursed are you above all livestock and all wild animals! You will crawl on your belly and you will eat dust all the days of your life.

15. And I will put enmity between you and the woman, and between your offspring and hers; he will crush your head, and you will strike his heel."

16. To the woman he said, "I will make your pains in childbearing very severe; with painful labor you will give birth to children. Your desire will be for your husband, and he will rule over you."

17. To Adam he said, "Because you listened to your wife and ate fruit from the tree about which I commanded you, 'You must not eat from it,' "Cursed is the ground because of you; through painful toil you will eat food from it all the days of your life.

18. It will produce thorns and thistles for you, and you will eat the plants of the field.

> 19 By the sweat of your brow you will eat your food until you return to the ground, since from it you were taken; for dust you are and to dust you will return."
>
> 20 Adam named his wife Eve, because she would become the mother of all the living.
>
> 21 The LORD God made garments of skin for Adam and his wife and clothed them.
>
> 22 And the LORD God said, "The man has now become like one of us, knowing good and evil. He must not be allowed to reach out his hand and take also from the tree of life and eat, and live forever."
>
> 23 So the LORD God banished him from the Garden of Eden to work the ground from which he had been taken.
>
> 24 After he drove the man out, he placed on the east side[e] of the Garden of Eden cherubim and a flaming sword flashing back and forth to guard the way to the tree of life.

I've highlighted verses 14-24 because they outline the curse. Let's examine them: starting in verse 14 we see that the serpent is cursed above all live-stock and every beast of the field, it will go upon its belly and shall eat dust all the days of its life (meaning it is the lowest of the low… subservient). If you think about a snake it actually slithers on the ground. In Verse 15, God has declared that satan and satan's seed and the woman and the woman's seed (mankind) will be enemies. He will crush your head and you will strike his heel…here is a foreshadow of pain. This passage points to Christ's delivering the deathblow to Satan by his redemptive work on the cross but Christ was also bruised.

Isaiah 53:4-5 says it best:

> "Surely he hath borne our griefs, and carried our sorrows: yet we did esteem him stricken, smitten of God, and afflicted. But he was wounded for our transgressions, he was bruised for our iniquities: the chastisement of our peace was upon him; and with his stripes we are healed.

Take a moment to really think about all that Christ suffered. It may be hard to imagine it exactly if you've never seen anyone flogged but the movie *Passion of the Christ* portrayed it better than many of the other movies about Jesus; you can really see all of the beatings and scourging that Christ suffered. Imagine being nailed to a board, just having someone hammer nails through your hands and feet is bad enough but then nailing those to a board and stand the board up.... just thinking about that is painful.

Verse 16 is when mankind's pain is outlined, the King James Version says I will greatly multiply thy sorrow and thy conception, pain in childbirth, pain in relationships, pain feeding yourself, the ground is cursed it will bring forth pain (thorns and thistles), pain taking care of yourself (in the sweat of thy face shalt thou eat bread) if you look at verse 21 when God made coats of skins, that's pain because that meant an animal had to be killed to clothe them. Adam also ultimately lost privileges and responsibility, and he and Eve were kicked out of their home. Disobedience brought about all of this pain; the entire creation was cursed; mankind, animals, and the earth. Look at Romans 8:20

20 For the creature was made subject to vanity, not willingly, but by reason of him who hath subjected the same in hope

21 Because the creature itself also shall be delivered from the bondage of corruption into the glorious liberty of the children of God. 22 For we know that the whole creation groaneth and travaileth in pain together until now.

Even Jeremiah asked God in Jeremiah 12:4:

"How long shall the land mourn, and the herbs of every field wither for the wickedness of them that dwell therein? The beasts are consumed, and the birds; because they said, He shall not see our last end." KJV

Many times pain stems from disobedience or lack of obedience. Take a look at Deuteronomy 28. Amazingly enough verses 1-14 talk about blessings of obedience but the next 53 verses (15-68) talks about the consequences of disobedience. This lets you know how serious God is about obedience; not only in the Old Testament but in the New Testament as well. These consequences or curses are broken into three groups of punishment: internal calamities (death, despair, disease, and decline); external judgment (defeat before the enemy) and the transmission of judgment to your descendants.

Let me clarify that the consequences in Deuteronomy were given to Moses when the children of Israel were wandering in the wilderness. They were under the law and were judged by the law, which meant you break the law (sin) the consequence is death. Christ came to fulfill the law and when you accept Him you are saved by grace. So right now you are either living in Adam's fallen nature, and living a death sentence, separated from God and under the curse of disobedience or you have accepted Christ as your redeemer, and have life, reconciled to God and living under grace.

Which are you? It's important that you know your status because it may have a lot to do with why you're experiencing pain.

We don't have to go all the way back to biblical days to see the consequences of disobedience, many times we can look at our own lives and trace it. Sin is sin and God is no respecter of persons. No matter who you are, if you are not obedient you will suffer the consequences of your disobedience. Many times you can bring a lot of suffering upon yourself. Believe me, I've been there and done that.

I was reassigned to Italy in September 1999. I had submitted to my call and had preached at a church in Louisiana before going to Italy. I knew that God had taken me to Italy to start my ministry. My daughter didn't go with me so I would only be in Italy for two years. I made a commitment to really study to show myself approved and seek God. I was totally dedicated to living holy and walking circumspectly before the Lord, for an entire week. A week after I arrived in Italy I met my now second ex-husband. We lived in a hotel right across from each other's. He walked into the housing office when I was waiting to go on a housing tour. We spoke but I was leaving for the tour. Later that evening I was walking back from dinner at a restaurant and he asked me about the housing tour. We talked until 5:30 the next morning and ended then only because he had to go to work. From that day on he basically moved into my hotel room. I would still read my word and pray but I didn't feel right. I've always been either in or out I can't be a hypocrite. I found a house a month later and although I'd also found him an apartment he moved into the house with me. I had never lived or as we call it in the South, shacked up with a man in my life and here I was in Italy supposedly to do the Lord's work and I was shacking with a man.

My ex was really a very responsible and thoughtful man. I remember for the first month of our relationship receiving a gift from him almost 5 times a week and even later into the relationship he would give me gifts and surprises; he handled his money well. He was everything that my first ex-husband was not so I was very caught up in the relationship. I loved him and really enjoyed being with him. He was very laid back and easy going. We never had an argument. We did have disagreements but we always talked them out giving each other respect. Our relationship was fantastic and I felt like the luckiest girl in the world.

My grandmother died a week after I'd gotten married. The military paid for me, my husband, and daughter to go home for the funeral/memorial. Despite the sadness of my grandmother's passing, we had a great time. He got to meet the rest of my family, see where I grew up and my favorite haunts as a teenager. Everything appeared to be really great. We flew back to Italy and was met at the airport by our neighbor; he dropped our car off to us and caught a ride home with his wife. On our way home, all hell broke loose. I told my ex to take a different route home because traffic was very heavy at that time of day. He got off of the interstate, pulled into a parking lot and got out of the car and walked away. I didn't see where he'd gone. I was really surprised and stunned, I didn't know what had happened. I sat there tired and stunned for almost 30 minutes before getting out to get into the driver's seat to go home. He suddenly materialized and got into the car. I got back in on the passenger side. He started the car and said to me, "don't you say an F__ing word to me". I was in a state of shock. Here was this man that I'd just married that I'd been dating for almost a year and a half, who had never raised his voice at me, we'd never had an argument or serious disagreement before but just because I was trying to keep us from sitting in traffic for two hours, he had totally disrespected me, with my daughter in the back seat. By the time we got home we were actually physically fighting; throwing blows.

The marriage went downhill from there. I realized that this man that I'd married was indeed a wolf in sheep's clothing. As a matter of fact all of the horrible things that were prophesied to me came true. He was not who I thought he was, the true him had finally shown up. His representative could not play the role any longer. Everything that I treasured in our relationship had been built on lies. I was truly out of my league. I had never had anyone deceive and manipulate me so fully. I had never had anyone talk to me so harshly and cruelly before. He would say the ugliest things to me and then apologize so smoothly. This didn't happen all of the time but one time was one time too many. What he said to me never hurt me because before I met him I was firm in who and what I was. There was nothing that he could say that would make me feel less than a person or doubt myself; my mom had done a really good job of affirming me. I was hurt that he had deceived me and that he could say such mean and ugly things to me. It changed me and made me angry. I would spend a lot of time thinking of ways to lash back out at him and truthfully I really wanted to do him bodily harm. The love that had started to grow for him began to die rapidly because I felt so deceived and tricked. I started hating him. Seeing his face made me sick to my stomach, watching him eat made me sick, everything about him repulsed me. He was extremely, verbally abusive and probably had been physically abusive in his other relationships.

That first fight was the only fight that we had because although he was crazy self-preservation was important too. I am almost 6'2 and I am what they call big boneded (I know it's not a word but that's how we say it in the South) I wrestled and fought with my brothers, I do not play anybody putting their hands on me. When we argued he would just say really ugly things and try to get in my face. He would look like a rabid dog, foaming at the mouth and just barking. At first I would argue with him but I'm not a barker, I'm a biter. I would listen to what he'd say for only so long before I bit him. This was really crazy. I would call the police to our house because I would be so angry I'd want them to come get me before I killed him. I remember once after he'd had surgery and I'd fixed him something to eat he took the plate and threw it against the wall. That enraged me. I was so enraged that somehow his shoulder got dislocated. I called the police because I could not get my anger under control. When they came they tried to calm me down and told him to go into the bedroom and lock the door. Another time he'd barked so much until I snapped and went after him with an axe. He locked the bedroom door and I began to chop into it to get to him. After things calmed down I slept with the axe by my side of the bed for weeks. I was able to sleep really peacefully, I don't even think he snored those weeks.

I left him or moved him out a couple of times but having another marriage fail was not appealing to me so I would always come back or let him come back. I remember one of the times I actually went out and got an apartment but I didn't stay one night because he knew all of the right things to say to make me come back home. I wasn't in that apartment for more than 5 minutes but we paid $5,000 because I'd already signed the lease. The truth was I saw a failed marriage as failure in me. I figured I was smart enough and brilliant enough to make a marriage work. My first failed marriage had really taken a toll on me because my first husband was my first love. I just couldn't believe that I could not make a marriage work. Don't get me wrong I understood that it takes two people to make a marriage work but I felt that if one of those people was me the odds were that much greater for success. I was devoted to making the marriage work. Not devoted to the man or really even wanting to be married to him but I was devoted to redeeming myself. Another reason that I didn't leave is because even though God had said no, I had asked Him to give me the man. I felt like I owed it to God to see it through. I had made my bed so I had to lie in it. This is the dumbest logic that you can have.

Although my ex-husband's words didn't affect me, they affected my daughter. She was 12 when he and I got married and had only seen me in a relationship with her father, my first ex. We never argued and he never, ever said a mean word to me. She had never experienced this so it would be very disturbing to her when he and I had an altercation. The first couple of times that we argued, she actually started screaming. There were even times that she thought he would hurt me and she would get very angry. Once she ran out of the house without any shoes on, jumped in her car and drove to the mall in tears. She worked in the mall at the time so she went to her friends for comfort.

My ex and I were married for 11 long, crazy years. We made good money and bought a lot of things. Life was very comfortable and I was able to give my daughter most of the things that she wanted but what I should have given her was a different life. We had really good times but also really bad times. Many times the bad overshadowed the good so much until it got harder and harder to remember the good.

Before meeting my ex I can say that I never regretted any of the decisions that I'd made even if some of them weren't the best decisions but I regret with all of my heart that I was disobedient to God and married him. I became someone that I didn't know; I learned how to hate and to distrust people. I learned a lot of things about myself that I never wanted to learn. Not only was my life turned upside down but so was my daughter's life. By the time the marriage ended we both needed therapy. My daughter chose not to go because she was just happy that he was no longer a part of our lives. She was 22 years old by then. I had so much anger built up in me that I knew I had to go.

Many times we cause our own pain. I brought a lot of pain into my own life through disobedience. Instead of just trusting God and postponing the marriage, I tried to fix it and bargain with God. This was unnecessary pain. This was not suffering for righteousness sake, this was suffering because I thought I knew more and could see further than my Creator. So I leaned to my own understanding and made a real mess of a lot of things.

I won't pretend that I have all of the answers to why you experience pain; I would not be foolish enough to claim that I know the mind of God. If you are saved and living under grace, some of your pain and suffering is inevitable so that God can get the glory out of your life and bring others to Christ. Remember Tyler Perry, his pain helped millions. I'm sure it was very unpleasant for him to experience the pain but it didn't kill him it only made him stronger and more appreciative of the blessings that he's received.

2 Timothy 3:12

"Yea, and all that will live godly in Christ Jesus shall suffer persecution" (KJV)

1 Peter 4:12-13:

12 Dear friends, do not be surprised at the fiery ordeal that has come on you to test you,

as though something strange were happening to you.

13 But rejoice inasmuch as you participate in the sufferings of Christ, so that you may be overjoyed when his glory is revealed.

If you are not saved and living under grace, there can be many reasons for your pain the ultimate one being that you are at the mercy of the enemy. He can do as he pleases with you because he is your father and you serve him.

John 8:44

42 Jesus said to them, "If God were your Father, you would love me, for I have come here from God. I have not come on my own; God sent me.

43 Why is my language not clear to you? Because you are unable to

hear what I say.

> ⁴⁴ You belong to your father, the devil, and you want to carry out your father's desires. He was a murderer from the beginning, not holding to the truth, for there is no truth in him. When he lies, he speaks his native language, for he is a liar and the father of lies.

Satan's main goal is to kill, steal and destroy. He hates God's love for all mankind and does all that he can to get the glory for himself. He will use anybody for his evil purposes and destroy them when he no longer needs them. Don't disillusion yourself into thinking that if you are not saved or if you don't bother Satan he won't bother you, that is not true the curse included all mankind not only those that choose salvation in Christ. Satan is the enemy to all mankind; there are no exceptions.

1 Peter 5:8 puts it best:

> ⁸ Be alert and of sober mind. Your enemy the devil prowls around like a roaring lion looking for someone to devour.

Satan has access to those that are not covered under the blood of Jesus but he cannot touch God's servant without permission. When Satan wanted to tempt Job he had to ask God's permission because Job was perfect, and upright, and one that feared God, and eschewed evil. He was under God's protection.

Job 1:8-12

> ⁸ Then the Lord said to Satan, "Have you considered my servant Job? There is no one on earth like him; he is blameless and upright, a man who fears God and shuns evil." ⁹ "Does Job fear God for nothing?" Satan replied. ¹⁰ "Have you not put a hedge around him and his household and everything he has? You have blessed the work of his hands, so that his flocks and herds are spread throughout the land. ¹¹ But now stretch out your hand and strike everything he has, and he will surely curse you to your face." ¹² The Lord said to Satan, "Very well, then, everything he has is in your power, but on the man himself do not lay a finger." Then Satan went out from the presence of the Lord.

Keeping these situations in mind, we will focus on pain that comes as a result of disobedience, poor decisions and choices, generational dysfunction and fear.

There are several definitions for pain:

a. the physical feeling caused by disease, injury, or something that hurts the body

b. mental or emotional suffering : sadness caused by some emotional or mental problem

c. someone or something that causes trouble or makes you feel annoyed or angry

d. a warning mechanism that helps protect us by influencing us to with- draw from harmful stimuli or situations.

Challenges of Being in Pain

I hurt my back in 2002. It was very strange the way that it happened. I'd just finished running about 6 laps and was leaving the track when I felt a horrible crushing feeling in my back that made me fall to my knees. I was in horrible pain. I had to go to the emergency room and get shots in my back. After having an MRI I found out that a disc in my back was bulging and sitting on my nerve. The pain from this was excruciating. That nerve runs down from your back through your butt cheek, hip, leg and into your foot. At any given time I was having pain in one or all of those areas. To try and alleviate the need for surgery, I went through traction, physical therapy, electronic impulses, everything. I was very upset about the back problems not only because of the pain and discomfort but because of how much it limited my ability to do the things that I wanted to do. I lived in Italy when this happened and I had been doing a lot of traveling throughout Europe and had plans to catch the trains and just trek from country to country. I wasn't able to do this because sitting for long periods of time was very painful and stressful on my body.

My back pain took a toll on my life, my family and my marriage. After all of the pain management techniques failed I decided to have surgery. My surgery was in March of 2003. After surgery I was very dependent on my husband and daughter to do a lot of things for me. This was a first; normally I was the one taking care of them but now they had to take care of me. I will admit I was not a good patient but I never felt like they really wanted to help. This caused me to be very irritable and moody and not really want their help. My mother had to come and take care of me. My mother is a great caretaker and having her there made things a lot easier for the whole family. The major problem that I faced is that although I'd had surgery, my pain didn't stop, it didn't even lessen; it actually got worse. I went from not being able to sit for long periods of time to not being able to sit at all. My butt hurt really badly; I felt like I was sitting on my bone. Most of the time I couldn't walk or if I did I would be limping. When I got well enough to do things for myself I'd try to shop at Walmart and would have to use the motorized chair. I was humiliated. My mother gave me a pep talk before I went to Walmart but having to be in that chair was too much. Dealing with the pain was one thing but the hardest thing was keeping my mind intact. My life had changed so drastically; I had gone from being very independent to being dependent on others. It was very hard to feel positive every single day and sometimes I'd let my pity party overtake me.

There were many changes in my life because I had to be conscious of my limitations and try not to overdo but I would always overdo. I like a spotless house it doesn't have to stay that way, but I want it to start out that way. We hired someone to come in and clean but I also wanted to clean because it was important to me that my family had a super clean house. I would spend hours cleaning on Saturdays; wiping down baseboards, scrubbing tile floors on my hands and knees, reaching into the cracks and crevices removing every bit of dust and dirt. Afterwards the house would look and smell completely fresh and new but I wouldn't be able to get out of bed for three days. Another change that was overwhelming to me was weight gain. I gained 60 pounds from inactivity. I love to eat. My mother, grandmother and aunts were really good cooks so mealtimes were always my favorite times. I was always very active so gaining weight was never a problem for me. I was so conditioned to eating what I want, when I want that I continued eating this way. Needless to say the pounds just kept piling on. This really caused me a lot of stress because I took great pride in the way my body looked, my lack of much body fat and being able to wear body hugging clothes. I had to buy clothes that were 4 sizes larger. I didn't feel sexy anymore. As a matter of fact, I didn't enjoy shopping and stopped doing it. I refused to buy size 16 and 18 clothes. I'm tall so I could hide weight well but I was really big. I didn't realize how big until I started to look at pictures.

During this time our financial status didn't change because I was in the military so I still received my full check but my relationship with my husband changed. It was not a very good relationship but I didn't really understand why it was changing because he really wasn't a very active guy and even with all of my pain I still was more active than he was. As I look back at it I think he was just so angry with God about my back problems that he couldn't see me straight anymore. When I hurt my back I was a minister in my church, preaching, teaching, and praying for others. My husband couldn't understand how God would heal others through me and not heal me. I'm not married to him anymore but whenever we have a need to talk, he always asks me about my back and says he is still so concerned about it.

I had a second back surgery in 2008 and I basically got my life back. That was five years after the first one and I will admit that those were five really challenging and trying years. My second surgery was a success. My disc had completely collapsed so the surgeon had to go in and remove it and put in a plate and screws. I am so much better this time. I experience pain from time to time and have episodes but most of the time I am at 80% and can do a lot of things that I enjoy. Praying and keeping my mind is the only thing that got me through this.

Many times mental and physical pain goes hand in hand. If you are hurting physically it can cause your lifestyle to change which may affect you mentally and emotionally. If you were the breadwinner or caregiver for your family you may have to share more of that responsibility with other family members which may cause resentment and even anger from them. This sharing the load may make you feel limited, worthless and like a burden to your loved ones because you are unable to do a lot of things that you did before. If you are the sole breadwinner and you become physically unable to work and aren't receiving any type of financial assistance or aide to continue the lifestyle that you are accustomed to living it also affects you mentally and emotionally.

When you are experiencing mental and emotional issues they may manifest into physical issues as well. If you are over stressed or anxious you can start having headaches, sore throat, muscle stiffness, aches, and insomnia, among other things. Even taking some of the prescribed medicines for depression and anxiety can cause liver, kidney, and other problems. Earlier when we talked about coping mechanisms, we talked about somatization. This is many times what happens when we are dealing with issues that overwhelm us.

If someone or something is causing you pain, you need to take a moment to figure out what purpose that person is serving in your life and in your move toward your purpose. Sometimes people work in our lives to make us uncomfortable with where we are so that we can reach for something better. This may be a supervisor that constantly rides you or a teacher or friend that's always challenging you. We don't always like the way they make us feel and they may cause us pain but it may be for your good. There's a difference between challenging and stretching and abusing or misusing. If someone is abusing or misusing you God is not using them to propel you into your purpose. They are there to kill, steal and destroy.

The type of pain that causes us to withdraw from harmful stimuli or situations is actually good for us. It helps keep us safe and sane. This pain hones our instincts and helps us recognize when we are in danger or keeps us from making the same mistakes over and over again. Everything has purpose even our pain. It's imperative that we don't allow our pain to stop us from living a full and successful life. When the bible talks about trials and testing they are only for a season; they don't last forever. If you read the Old Testament you will see that the Israelites went through highs and lows, mountains and valleys. That's how our lives will be. How can you be a light on a hill and the salt of the earth drawing people to Christ which is your great commission if you are always broken and hurting? The prescription is to press your way and to endure until the end. Go through the storm...get through the pain, don't get stuck in it. No one that served Christ escaped persecutions. Every person we read about in the bible, no matter how God loved them, went through some form of trial. We have a high priest that understands what we are going through because he was tempted and tested.

Regardless of the type of pain we experience and even if it works to make us better, stronger or smarter, it can still lead to depression, disassociation and possibly even suicide. So what do we do to decrease and possibly alleviate the physical, mental and emotional pain that we experience? I'm glad that you asked. We are going to do something very simple, as a matter of fact you learned this in kindergarten..... Stop, Look and Listen. I was kind of skeptical about putting this exercise in this book because some men may not see it as being very manly and may not be able to get the benefit of it. I changed my mind because I was giving a male friend a massage the other day and he had tension in every part of his body. Not only that but if I didn't just force the issue he would not have gotten what he needed; rest and relaxation. Before I began the massage, I put on soothing classical and jazz music and he fell asleep immediately. When I talked to him the next day he said that he'd slept better and woke up feeling better than he'd felt in years. I know that men are being more open about pampering themselves, I'm seeing more and more men when I go to get a pedicure and to the salon but it's important that you are re-energized so that you are more effective for God, yourself and all of the people that rely on you. It's important to remember that even God rested on the 7th day of creation. I won't even get into what day of the week that was but I will remind you that if an all-powerful God needed to rest so do you. So take your time and enjoy.

Stop – Life can feel like it's crowding in on you when there are so many things that need your attention. What happens at these times is you don't take the time to stop and listen to God. As a matter of fact I don't know many men that spend a lot of time alone, with everything turned off and just sit and meditate. I know this sounds like a self-help book but the truth is to get anything in perspective sometimes you have to turn everything off so you can tune in. So Stop, turn off everything, sit in a very comfortable place and take a deep breath…. exhale….. do it again because you didn't do it right the first time. This time focus on breathing….. inhale… your chest should rise and it should feel a little strained because you may not really do this often… exhale…. do this three more times or until it doesn't feel forced. Let your head fall down, chin on your chest and sit that way for five minutes, breathing deeply…. let your head fall back and side to side 1 minute in each position and take deep breaths. Next hold out your hands and stretch your fingers out wide and take each finger down one at a time…. get a good stretch. Just sit there for 10 more minutes just thinking about moving your head, fingers, shoulders or whatever other body part you want to stretch. Don't let your mind wander to anything else. After 10 minutes are up, let's move to Look.

Look – I want you to close your eyes and take a good look at yourself. See a picture of yourself in your mind. Look at all of the issues that you have to deal with, as a matter of fact, stack all of the issues in the corner of the picture. You can make as many stacks in the picture as you want but never lose sight of you in the picture, if you have to widen the frame that's okay just ensure that you can see yourself. After you finish your stacks, I want you to go through and prioritize your issues. After you finish prioritizing hold the top three issues in your hand. Take your foot and push the stack(s) of other issues out of the frame completely. You should only be able to see yourself in the picture, holding no more than three issues in your hand (if you have less that's not a problem, that's actually great). Next, picture God, in whatever way you imagine him, in the picture with you. Take the first issue and I want you to tell God about it. Start at the beginning and tell him every single thing that you can think of about this issue, don't hold anything back. After you tell him everything, take that issue and hand it over to him. Do the same thing for the next two issues. Say everything that you want to say to him about the issues. After you are finished take a deep breath and let's move to listen.

Listen – With your eyes still closed. I want you to sit still and listen to God. Many Christians don't know God's voice because they are either too busy, talk constantly or can't recognize God's voice. We have to train our ears and hearts to hear God's voice. So I want you to sit quietly. If any random thoughts come to mind, and they are going to, I just want you to say I hear you Lord and get refocused. The first couple of times that you sit to listen you may not hear anything that you believe is God's voice but the more you talk to Him and listen for His voice your ear will become trained to hear Him and eventually you won't even have to sit still to hear.

This **Stop-Look-and Listen** exercise should be done daily or any time you feel overwhelmed or anxious. God wants to be a part of your life. He is concerned about everything that concerns you but many times we are so busy stressing that we're not busy hearing. Take time to hear from God and seek Him for guidance. If he created you for a purpose, He knows what that purpose is and if you allow Him to He will lead you into the path of purpose.

I Peter 5:6-7

6 Humble yourselves, therefore, under God's mighty hand, that he may lift you up in due time.

7 Cast all your anxiety on him because he cares for you.

Remember.... Even your pain has purpose so don't despise it. Pray and get through it because your Father in heaven is there with you, He sees you and He knows how to ensure that all things work together for your good, doesn't derail your purpose and gives you a future and a hope.

CHAPTER 4

Exposure

In the past two chapters, we've discussed dealing with your past and pain. Now that you've had an opportunity to really examine past situations, experiences and hurts and the way that they have affected your present life it's time to start the healing process by putting those past things behind you.

Two big steps to overcome your past is to own it and to forgive.

Owning it means accepting that what happened did happen to you. You can't forget or pretend your way out of it. It happened. Owning it brings it to the light where it is exposed. Exposure speeds up the healing process. We use the expression bring it to light or brought to light when something is exposed because when it's covered, it's hidden, it's in darkness. Exposing it uncovers it. When you are in Christ you no longer walk in darkness, God has called you out of darkness into His marvelous light. This means that everything that is hidden in your life must be brought into light; must be uncovered. Although God knows what lies underneath, in darkness, you still need to expose yourself to Him. When you do that is your way of telling God I trust you, I am naked before you, baring everything to you so you can heal me.

Men don't normally expose themselves to anyone. They are like players in a poker game. They keep a straight face, hold their hand close and strategize based on the other player's move. Even when men are caught in compromising positions they will not immediately come clean. Think about all of the scandals that have happened in the last 20 years. The man denies, denies, denies, even when the evidence is stacked high against him, still denial. This reminds me of a joke that Eddie Murphy told on Raw about a woman seeing her husband coming out of another woman's house and when she asked him about it the conversation went like this:

"What was you doing in that lady's house?" He said, "Wasn't me."

She said, "I looked right in your face." He said "Wasn't me."

She said, "I'm supposed to be a fool right?" He said, "Hey, wasn't me."

She looked at him and said "You know what, maybe it wasn't you."

I paraphrased a little bit because Eddie Murphy was really raw on Raw. It was quite obvious that he was angry, bitter and hurt. Instead of sitting down with the person that had broken his heart or with a therapist and try to make sense of what he was feeling he got on stage and made jokes about his pain. I don't know Eddie so I can't speak for him. Maybe this was a cathartic way for him to deal with pain but many times people, men especially, laugh to keep from crying.

We talked about Tyler Perry in the last chapter and how his pain and suffering brought about success and helped millions of people but what I didn't mention was how he came from behind the camera and in an interview with Oprah exposed himself to the world. His story of physical and sexual abuse helped many men because it freed them to come forward. I'm sure that was not an easy thing for him to do. Think about it, he exposed himself to the world, not just to his girlfriend or wife or to a therapist that's sworn to secrecy but to any and everybody that was listening. That interview can be replayed again and again. He was freed that day. There is healing in exposure. It may not feel like it at first but in time you will feel liberated and free. You don't have to go around exposing yourself to the world like Tyler did, as a matter of fact after God, the next person that you need to expose yourself to is to you. There are some things that you need to acknowledge to yourself.

It's time that you uncover yourself and get naked. I will go first to show you how it's done. I want you to know that everything inside of me screams at the thought of exposing myself to you but it is for our good because it is only when truth comes out that we are free.

Hello my name is Reneé and I am a cheater.

I have never been faithful in a relationship. I hate to admit this especially since I have had such wonderful men in my life and I want them to know, if they are reading this book, that it was the dysfunction in me and not the lack in them that caused me to be unfaithful.

I think I felt the impact of being a cheater after my second ex-husband cheated on me. It was quite ironic that he would cheat because I had never cheated on him. Well let me put that another way, I hadn't cheated on the third person in our marriage covenant... God. My ex I could care less about cheating on but I did not want to disappoint God and I was very serious when I made that covenant. It was never my intent to be a cheater and I didn't want to hurt anyone but hurting people hurt people. I know you've heard this before but it's true. Think about your life and how many people you've hurt, be honest with yourself, no excuses. How many times have you gone out and gotten with someone else when you were still reeling from the last relationship? How many times have you left one woman's bed just to go to another woman's bed? How many booty calls have you made when you know that your willing partner secretly wants your days and nights and is only settling for the booty call? How many "lil something, somethings" on the side do you have?

I've spent years studying men and their habits because I have always had so many male friends and I've watched my three younger brothers grow up and navigate relationships. I hung out with guys so much that I became like one of the guys. Cheating was easy. Sex and love were two completely different things to me and I could definitely have sex without the love. As a matter of fact sins of the flesh are the hardest to overcome. I talk about this extensively in my book, Killer Sex, Do Not Be Deceived so I won't elaborate much here.

My first base was in Shemya Alaska. This 2x5 island is in the Aleutian Islands, about 1,500 miles from Anchorage Alaska. When I arrived in 1987 there were about 500 men and about 23 women. 98% of the women lived in the same dormitory area. I was the youngest person on the island at 18 years old. When I looked back on it, I don't think it was the best assignment for someone as young and new to the Air Force as I was. I learned a lot about my job, was able to get the needed training and to go to college because there wasn't much else to do on the island. What there was time to do and I majored in was to learn about the dynamics between men and women, particularly since there were so many men to choose from, and to discover sex.

When I discovered sex I fell in love with it immediately. I loved everything about it; the feel of a man's body on mine how he's hard in places where I'm soft; the slightly rough texture of his hands as they run across my body; the labored breathing; how we'd inhale and exhale on a single breath; the hungry kisses…. Ok I think you get the picture… moving right along. I didn't only discover sex I also discovered porn. I'd never watched a porn movie before but one of the guys that I knew had an extensive library. I would actually watch porn every day and would always want to practice the moves that I saw. I had many willing guinea pigs to help in my research and try out these new moves. I was fascinated with all things sexual and developed a very clinical approach to sex. I didn't have to feel anything for the subject my goal was to perfect the position or recreate the response that I saw on the screen. Needless to say this was not only ungodly but extremely unhealthy. Oversaturation from the porn and sexual experimentation caused me to be emotionally detached from the sex act and I always felt like something was missing so I was never really satisfied.

When I left Shemya, I requested to be stationed at home in Louisiana. After I got there I married my high school sweetheart and we started our lives together. I loved him and I was very excited about our future. Our sex life was great. We could never get enough of each other particularly when I was pregnant. We could barely make a 3 hour trip to Dallas without having to pull over on the side of the road for loving. Things were great and I was very happy but that was not to last. We were not able to weather the storms and tornadoes that wreaked havoc in our marriage. When my husband and I separated my life of cheating began.

When you're in the military you are kind of in a closed society so you feel relatively safe meeting and dating other military people. Working in such close proximity to men made it easy for me to meet other men. I never wanted to date anyone that I worked with because it could cause conflict.

Like I told you in Chapter 2, when my marriage fell apart my heart was cold and I felt empty. Only what I wanted mattered to me. If I was in a relationship with someone and I started being interested in someone else I would just start seeing that other person, never even bothering to end the other relationship. I was very open, I wouldn't care if the person I was in a relationship with saw me with other men. If they asked me questions about it I would always be honest with them and give them the choice to continue seeing me or move on. If they agreed to continue the relationship I would see them both until one of them began to profess love and pressure me for monogamy. I would appear flattered but would be feverishly thinking of ways to end the relationship; which I would do immediately. The really bad thing about it all is that I didn't appear cold and heartless. As a matter of fact I came across very loving. I would make whoever I was with feel extremely loved and cherished. I would be in deep, all-consuming love until someone else caught my eye.

I was sick so I prescribed alcohol and sex to make me feel better. That was a lethal combination because both of those things impair your judgment and good sense. I didn't think about hurting others I just did what I wanted to do. In my mind, what I was doing had nothing to do with whoever I was with. My feelings for them didn't change, I was just doing my thing. After a couple of the guys that I'd dumped came apart on me I realized that I needed to incorporate full disclosure at the beginning of the relationship. I would tell them that I wasn't interested in monogamy and that it was okay if they saw other people because I was going to. Those relationships would start out great and the guy would say he could handle it but sooner or later he would demand monogamy or come to me with the great love and marriage confession. I would immediately end the relationship. When relationships started overwhelming me, I'd have one night stands. I'd pick a guy out in the club and tell him he was going home with me. This was very dangerous but I was living dangerously anyway. I had affairs with married men and felt like I was doing their wives a favor. I felt that they were going to cheat anyway and if they cheated with me I would keep their home intact because I was never interested in full-time. I had already been full-time and that had failed.

I struggled with this lifestyle for a few years. It wasn't easy for me to live this way because I knew God. When I was living this way, I would attend church off and on, and would even decide to turn from my backslidden ways but that would not last. It's hard to change outwardly when inwardly you're still broken. If you don't get to the root of the sickness you will continue to have symptoms. What really helped me was when my drinking began to really get out of control. I despise addiction and I'd seen the effects of alcoholism in my family. So when I realized that I was becoming addicted to drinking, I quit immediately. Went completely cold turkey. This helped me to think clearer and I began to make changes in my life.

In 1998, I decided it was time for me to stop living a fast life and really turn back to the Lord. I knew that what I was doing was wrong and that God was very displeased with me. I stopped everything and began to seek God for my life. I had known that I had a call on my life and I didn't want to die in my sin and not do what God created me to do. Plus, I really was never satisfied. I was looking for satisfaction in a bottle and sex but I could never find it there because only God could satisfy the emptiness that I had. God was the true satisfier of my soul.

Two years later, when I was going through my deliverance session God exposed my sins to me one night. After I'd prayed and laid down to sleep,

I began to see the faces of every man that I'd ever had sex with. I thought I was dreaming so I opened my eyes, but they were still there, one by one flashing in and out before me. I could only lie there and endure the haunting of my past. I began to feel sick and nauseous. I was ashamed, some of the faces I couldn't even put a name to. I couldn't turn away I was forced to behold the sins of my past. At this point I had developed a sensitivity to sin so this was real torture for me. The next morning when I woke up I felt different. I felt lighter than I had in years. I felt clean like I had been washed on the inside from head to toe. The Lord brought the night to my remembrance and told me that He had purged me and cleansed me from all unrighteousness. I had been washed in the blood of Jesus.

I was excited about my new life. I was delivered and healed. I felt whole and able to really be effective at what God had taken me to Italy to do. But despite the healing and cleansing I still had to pay the cost for the sinful life that I'd led. Galatians 6:7 reminds us:

> Be not deceived; God is not mocked: for whatsoever a man soweth, that shall he also reap.

I met my second ex-husband in Italy and got remarried in 2001. When my ex and I married I was only 31 years old and he was only 32. There was nothing that should have stood in the way of sexual bliss. When we would make love before we were married I felt convicted so that would always put a damper on things for me. I would repent and promise not to go there again but it was just a no win cycle. It was hard because our love making was very enjoyable; I was definitely excited about our marriage bed. I was looking forward to breaking out of that cycle. The night that we got married instead of going back to our house where my mom and daughter were we went to his apartment for privacy and to share our first night together as man and wife. That night we both had a lot of nervous energy so we just talked for several hours but did not consummate our marriage that night. I didn't know that was a sign of things to come.

After about a week, I noticed that we weren't having sex. We were still intimate: he'd kiss me when he walked into the house, we'd snuggle when we watched movies, and he'd hug me while I cooked or whenever he came upon me but no sex. My ex and I were both in college at the time. We worked during the day and alternated nights for class because someone had to be home with my daughter. At first I thought maybe the heavier school schedule was the cause of the problem; whoever went to class normally didn't get home until 9:30 or 10:00. I decided to take things into my own hands literally and tried to initiate sex on a weekend night but my ex said that he was tired and just turned away. Another week passed and I decided to mention it to him thinking that maybe we'd get a good laugh out of it and things would change. He told me that sex was all I ever thought about and that was the only reason that I'd married him. I was shocked because although that wasn't true what man would be upset about that. I continued to question him so that I could understand how he'd come to that conclusion. He never said anything that made any sense to me. I felt like I was being tested and tried (by fire). I was married to a man that had completely deceived me about who he was in every way. I had no idea who I was living with. What made it even worse is that I'd made commitments to God: I was going to preach and teach His word; I was going to honor my marriage covenant with Him and my husband; I was going to be loyal and faithful in everything.

I was living in hell. I slept next to a man in the same bed every night, who threw his legs and arms around me, I was basically cocooned by his body, and who snored and kept me awake. I was actually homicidal. I began to understand how people just snap and kill their spouses. I felt like I was experiencing psychological warfare and losing. I couldn't understand how a man could be that tired or have a headache that often. I was too vain to think that I didn't please him; after all I had plenty testimonies of my prowess as a lover. The few times that we had sex, I stopped calling it making love because there was absolutely no love in that bed, his enjoyment was so vocal that I was concerned that the neighbors would think that I was killing him. I thought maybe he was gay, after all I didn't know this guy, but I would see cybersex chat transcripts he'd have with other women. They were boring but he seemed interested enough in women. I talked to several of my male friends about it hoping that they could shed a little light on it for me. None of them could understand it either. One of my friends said that maybe he was sick. I made a doctor's appointment but besides putting on a little weight he was fine. One of my friends told me to find ways to spice things up more so that he'd be enticed enough to want to have sex. I went to an adult novelty store to find new and exciting things, I bought a couple of things and talked to the sales rep about the problem. He told me that lack of exercise can cause a low libido. Exercising didn't work. I also bought these pills that's supposed to increase your sexual appetite. I put that in his juice but that didn't work either.

This lack of sex was really beginning to take its toll on me because I was determined to be faithful to my covenant. I started being a workaholic and got involved in a lot of different events to take my mind off being angry and dissatisfied. I worked tirelessly in the church and would take on project after project. I would have dinner party after dinner party just to have other people around. The nights that I was at my breaking point I would try to touch my husband and force him to have sex but I just felt like I was raping him and that would make me physically sick. I finally gave up. I stopped being interested in him sexually, besides he may have graduated from cybersex to actual sex with other women and I wasn't interested in having an STD or HIV.

My husband retired from the military in August 2005. Our marriage wasn't really good and I could tell that we were growing further and further apart. I began to notice that he spent more time on the computer and he was being distant. I was too indifferent to care. I figured he wasn't putting out or meeting my needs so it didn't matter if he was unhappy, I was unhappy. In January 2006, he told me that he was going to Miami for some type of Photoshop Convention or other I really didn't care where he was going or why he was going. He went and came back after a week or so. I could tell something was different but I didn't even bother asking about it. In February he told me he was going back to Miami to look for work. I didn't even challenge that weak excuse I just agreed with whatever he wanted to do. The morning that he'd planned to leave I knew that he was leaving for good so I said goodbye and went to work. He called me at work later in the morning to say that he wasn't coming back. I wasn't surprised but I was upset that he would call me at work with such upsetting news because he knew that I had troops working for me and it was totally unprofessional to sit in my office crying over our nonsense. I let his words roll over me, hung up the phone and went back to work. That evening when I got home I called him to find out what was going on and he just gave me typical empty answers so I began to do a little researching and within an hour I knew the address to where he'd gone, the woman's name that he'd gone to be with, her phone number, where she worked, what her `license plate number was and the daycare that her daughter went to.

I couldn't believe that he'd left me for another woman. It was extremely ironic to me and I began to laugh. I'm sure my daughter thought I was having a nervous breakdown. The first man that I hadn't cheated on, had actually been faithful to although he had denied me my due benevolence, left me for another woman. Strangely enough my thinking was so off that I never considered the online cybersex as cheating but I saw this leaving to go be with another woman as just down right disloyalty. He left everything intact, my finances didn't change, he started all over again, I had everything; house, cars, his retirement check, savings. My life didn't miss a beat. Despite this I was extremely angry. I had to really pray to keep myself together because I wanted to just show up on their doorstep and wreak serious havoc. How dare I be a good, faithful wife to him and he leave me. Did he realize how hard it had been for me to deny myself sex for years because I was trying to be faithful. My flesh would even rise up and I would think don't he know who I am and how many other men I could have been sleeping with? I tried going out with other men but that didn't work because I had changed. I even set up a night of sex with an old boyfriend but I couldn't go through with it because I had been delivered. That old life was no longer appealing or possible for me.

I really grew closer to God during this time because my prayer life greatly increased. One day in my reading I came across Galatians 6:7 and realized that I'd sown a lot of corruption and that God's word is true, I would reap what I'd sown and I shouldn't be surprised when these things came upon me. God would help me make it through but I was going to go through it. My husband eventually came back in a month and told me why he'd left. For a couple of months he kept coming back and leaving only to finally return in May. Our marriage was over. It was really over before it started. We stayed together for 4 more years and finally in July 2010 it came to a screeching halt.

What do you need to expose? What do you need to call a spade? Take time and think about your life and what you have been making excuses for or calling by another name. I'm sure there may be many things that you need to deal with but many times we just use things to cover it up. That's where a lot of abuse stems from particularly alcohol and drug abuse. It's time to bring all of these things to the light. No more repressing, suppressing or coping. What happened to you may have been extremely horrible, extremely degrading, and extremely hurtful. What you might have done to others may have been extremely harsh, extremely hurtful or extremely humiliating but you can change it. Before you can change anything you must first acknowledge it. You can make it better because you are still here. You lived to tell the tale, you lived to affect other people's lives. Notice I said affect not infect. Although both words can have negative and positive meanings, when we think of infect it's normally negative. When we infect someone we think of giving them an infection or something that makes them sick, can hurt or kill them. So instead of spreading the germs of your past around you should take time to see the master physician so he can heal you of your sickness and deliver you from disease so your experiences can affect other people's lives in a positive way through identification, encouragement, and perseverance.

Let's shine the light of God's mercy and allow the Balm of Gilead to heal us.

Remember forgiveness is also necessary. It's important to forgive, if you don't forgive God won't forgive you but also if you don't forgive that hurt will be replicated again and again in your mind. When you hold something against someone every time they cross your mind or you see them that hurt is reawakened; you get angry, shame or flustered. It's a constant reminder of your pain or shame. Forgiving them helps you to release them and their actions from your mind, just let it go. I know this is not so easy to do especially if you feel like something was taken away from you or you were cheated out of a good life but you've owned it, you're still living and your future depends on you letting it go. It doesn't normally happen overnight it is a process but if you have a true desire to forgive God will help you.

As you expose yourself you need to also forgive yourself. Sometimes we are harsher on ourselves than we are on others even those that hurt and abuse us. I had to forgive myself. I did not feel good about cheating. I hurt a lot of people. When I talk to some of my girlfriends that have dealt with cheating husbands and I hear the pain in their voice I am reminded that I caused another woman that same kind of pain. When my guy friends tell me about a woman that has broken their heart, I am reminded that I broke hearts of many really good men. I apologized to those that I could and I prayed for those that I have lost contact with. I don't know what you have to forgive yourself for maybe it's for hurting others or maybe thinking that you deserved to be treated and misused if you were a victim of abuse. You may have to forgive yourself for making excuses for your abuser. Whatever forgiveness you need give it. Let go of the guilt. Uncover it all. Release it all. Let the light shine on you! Your health, self-image, and future depend on it.

CHAPTER 5

Who Am I?

Who Am I?

Turn and introduce yourself to the person sitting next to you. Start by saying, Hello I am……..

What did you tell the person about yourself?

In the last two lessons we've looked at our past, talked about situations we've experienced, our hurts and pain and exposed things that have affected our lives in many ways. In this chapter we will do damage control because many times we lose sight of who we are because we identify ourselves by our past, our pains, our roles, or our dysfunction. Think about how you introduced yourself. Did your past show up? For example if you were a drug user or your old profession, did you put that in your introduction? How about your marital status? Did you say I'm divorced or I'm single? Did any of your roles show up, i.e. I am a CEO or I play for this or that team? What about your dysfunction? I'm unemployed, I'm a recovering alcoholic, I'm depressed; did any of those things show up? Maybe you didn't say any of these things today when asked to introduce yourself but think about other times that you've introduced yourself to someone, what did you say?

I did speed dating. I was excited about it because I'd read testimonials about how fun and exciting it was. I suppose I was at the wrong session. The age group was 44-58. The women sat at tables and the men rotated. We had about 5 minutes to meet and talk with each other. If you were interested to get to know the person that you talked to better you would basically go to the speed dating site and select that person's number. Five minutes goes by very quickly but I was glad because instead of feeling like a single woman looking for a single man for friendship and fun I felt like a therapist.

I met 9 men most of them in their mid to late 50s. Each man that sat at my table started off by telling me his name, how long he'd been divorced, what had happened to end his marriage and what he did for a living. One of the guys who appeared to be in his early sixties told me a very sad tale about a hit and miss relationship that he'd had with a woman for years. They were never in the same state at the same time. She died before they were able to be together and it was quite obvious that he was still very sad about her death and the missed opportunity. That must have been a school night literally because 7 of the 9 men were either teachers or coaches and all but two of them were extremely sad. Their identity was wrapped up in their condition.

Most people spend their lives trying to answer the question Who Am I. The first glimpse that you get of yourself is through the eyes of your parents. They will build you up and make you feel good about who you are or they will tear you down and make you feel useless and worthless. Not only do their actions speak to you but also their inaction; their presence and their absence. Every encounter with your parents speaks to your value and worth. Unknowingly they began to shape you and create your identity from the moment you are taken out of the womb. What makes that so scary is that many times your parents are still trying to figure out who they are. How can they tell you who you are when they don't know who they are? It's hard to identify something when you're not sure of its origin; you don't know how to take care of it or meet its needs. This lack of identity is what tears down families; particularly in the African American community.

> In nothing was slavery so savage and relentless as in its attempted destruction of the family instincts of the Negro race in America. Individuals, not families; shelters, not homes; herding, not marriages, were the cardinal sins in that system of horrors. [4]
>
> FANNIE BARRIER WILLIAMS

Just as we have taken a look at our past to move through the bondage and pain of our experiences we must also take a look at history to see how our identity was shaped. We've discussed how our parents are the first identifiers for us but we must go back even further and see where this lack of identity in the African American community started. We must start from the beginning of the history that we know.

Many cultures have been affected by slavery, bondage or ethnic cleansing. What makes the African American experience so different is that slaves lost their names; many times first and last names. Losing your name is losing your identity and your history.

When we introduce ourselves the first information that we give is our name.

Back in biblical times names had significance and meaning; they normally related to current relation or prophecy from God. When God changed a person's position or identity he also changed their name. Abram is one example, he went from being Abram which means Exalted Father signifying his honor as progenitor or ancestor in the direct line to Abraham which means Father of A Great Multitude because God made him father of many nations. We do not practice this in our society today. First names don't have much meaning they are usually made up by the parents, chosen to honor a family member or just given. It's the last name that has significance in modern society.

Your last name connects you; it tells what family you are a part of either through blood or marriage and connects you to other families that are a part of your tree. Your last name also identifies your history. Unless through marriage, if your name is changed or taken away your history is also lost. It's hard to move forward if you can't accurately track your past. I'm not saying that it's impossible but it's hard. All of the slaves that came to America took on the last names of their slave owners. Think about that, adult men that had a name with a history attached to it were taken away from all that they knew and given another name. The new name was given to identify slaves as the property of the master with servitude, abuse, bondage, loss, and death attached to it. Not to use slavery as a crutch but to heal from anything you have to open up the wound completely and we do that by examining slavery and its effects on the African American race. Generation upon generation of African Americans can only trace their family history back to plantations in the South. There is no proud heritage for them there are only broken homes, broken dreams and broken lives. Pain is a common element; pain of loss, isolation, separation, and lost identity.

In one of my high school classes we had to research and write the history of our family along with a reconstruction of the coat of arms. A coat of arms or a family crest is a symbol of a family's identity and values. I was not eager to do this assignment because we had to present our reports to the class. I grew up in a small town where history was very important and your last name opened or closed doors for you. I knew that the largest part of my family history was filled with Caucasians and slave owners. At this time I was living in the city and was attending an all-black, private Catholic school. I didn't understand why my teacher asked us to do this assignment because everyone in the class could only trace their heritage back to a slave plantation and slave owner. We didn't have ancestry.com or other sites back then and no one in my class had made the trip back to the Motherland to figure out who their true ancestors were.

When the day came for me to stand in front of the class and do my report I wasn't very happy. Although none of the history was my fault there was something daunting about telling my classmates about that history. The town that I'd lived in most of my life actually celebrated and enshrined everything that had to do with history. It was the very first settlement in Louisiana and was very proud of that fact. Starting in 2nd grade I was taught the history of the town, the settlers and most of the plantations. So I knew and had made peace with my family's history but I didn't want to share it with my classmates. My heritage started at slavery almost immediately; my great great grandfather was a slave owner and the plantation still stood and was operational in the small town that I'd grown up in.

I was not proud of that heritage but I knew about it. I had been taught about it. This was my family's legacy. A legacy of pain perpetuated from generation to generation. Many African Americans don't know anything about a proud heritage. They can't look back and see anything good in past generations. There aren't many African American companies that have been passed down from generation to generation to generation. Even the contributions that we've made in modern day society are overlooked because we don't know anything about it; we were never taught about it. If you ask a student to name 10 African Americans whose contributions affect our lives every day, most could come up with 5 or 6, if you ask their parents they may come up with only 2 or 3. We are not interested in trying to grow together as a people because we are so divided. African Americans have learned everybody's history but our own so we don't know that we have much to be proud of.

Look at your parents are they living a lot better than you are? What about your grandparents and your great grandparents? What about other family members? How many of them lived or are living better than you live? Many times the answer to these questions is not many. Why? Because no one knew how to do any better because there was no example of better living and if there was it was seen as an affront to everyone else instead of something to celebrate. Think about the few people in your family that dared to live better. Were they celebrated or were they berated?

One of the reasons why the African American community is still so afflicted by slavery is because although slaves were freed physically, mentally many of them were still in bondage. A human mind can only take so much abuse and negative pummeling before it either breaks or believes what it's being fed. If someone is telling you day in and day out that you are worthless and have no value and everything around you lines up with that it won't take long before you begin to believe it. Once you believe it you conform to it, you become what they say you are; For as a man thinks in his heart; so is he. Mental bondage causes fear and paralyzes you. Instead of moving forward you stay in the same situation because fear is your constant companion. You are limited by accepting others' cruel words as your reality. You are imprisoned in your mind with the sturdiest bars and strongest chains and you are mightily bound.

Fear is very powerful. It makes you stay when everything in you screams to go or makes you go when you are supposed to stay. It makes the greatest orator sound like a blabbering idiot and the most talented individual an inept paraplegic. That's how powerful and paralyzing fear can be. Fear is not always overcome; even if your actions appear to not be governed by fear it can just be hidden down deep in your heart rearing its ugly head at any moment. If you live in fear for a long period of time it becomes your gauge; every decision you make or don't make, every action you take or don't take comes from that place of fear. We use other words to describe it: cautious, analytical, safe, or apprehensive but the truth is it's just plain old fear. A lot of your fear came from your parents; they passed it on to you like it was passed on to them and so forth and so on. Even Christians that go to church every week, recite scripture, and pray live in fear in some area of their lives.

Dr. Martin Luther King, Jr. is right when he said:

"As long as the mind is enslaved, the body can never be free. Psychological freedom, a firm sense of self-esteem, is the most powerful weapon against the long night of physical slavery. No Lincolnian emancipation proclamation or Johnsonian civil rights bill can totally bring this kind of freedom. The negro will only be free when he reaches down to the inner depths of his own being and signs with the pen and ink of assertive manhood his own emancipation proclamation. And, with a spirit straining toward true self-esteem, the Negro must boldly throw off the manacles of self-abegnation and say to himself and to the world, "I am somebody. I am a person. I am a man with dignity and honor. I have a rich and noble history, however painful and exploited that history has been. Yes, I was a slave through my foreparents, and now I'm not ashamed of that. I'm ashamed of the people who were so sinful to make me a slave." Yes, yes, we must stand up and say, "I'm black , but I'm black and beautiful." This, this self-affirmation is the black man's need, made compelling by the white man's crimes against him."[5]

That's why it's important that we look at how your identity was formed. That has a lot to do with where you are currently; how you feel about yourself, how you make decisions, how you value relationships, etc.

The first step we will take is to identify and root out fear. What fear runs through your family? What has held your family back generation after generation? What were your great, great grandparents afraid of? What were your grandparents afraid of? What were your parents afraid of? What are you afraid of? You may not think that you know or can come up with anything but think about what warnings you were given or what was an unwritten "family rule". Think about how money was handled, decisions were made and crises were dealt with, these are key areas that help you detect underlying fear. Other questions to determine where fear originated are: How did your parents grow up? Was it similar to how you grew up? If so, in what ways? If not, how was it different? Do you think your parents grew up in better or worse conditions than you grew up in? In what ways?

You may know the answer or be able to make a really good assumption so work with that first. Even after you make your assumption, talk to your family members to confirm your thoughts, you'll be surprised at what you don't know about your family. If you can't even make an assumption you need to ask your parents or grandparents to shed a little light on it for you.

Let's look at 2 Timothy 1:7 and discuss fear from a biblical perspective.

[7] For God hath not given us the spirit of fear; but of power, and of love, and of a sound mind.

You would think that fear would have started in Genesis 3:14-24 since that is when God is outlining the curse; but it doesn't. When God tells them that there will be enmity between the serpent's seed and the woman's seed He showed them the results of that enmity all the way to the end.....verse 15c ... "it shall bruise thy head, and thou shalt bruise his heel." There was nothing about living in fear from or fear of each other. Nowhere in the bible do you find that mankind (Eve's seed) should fear Satan. As a matter of fact fearing man is nowhere in the bible. The only person to be feared is God; fear as it relates to God is "to revere". The only time scripture admonishes us to fear God in more than a reverent way is in Matthew 10:28

> 28 And fear not them which kill the body, but are not able to kill the soul: but rather fear him which is able to destroy both soul and body in hell.

This scripture captures an Omnipotent or all powerful God. It lets you know that nothing that you fear is more absolute than destruction of your soul and body in hell and that only God has the authority to do that. Even Satan does not have that authority for he himself will one day be cast into everlasting fire. If you look at fear this way you can truly attest that there is nothing to fear but God.

Fear can cause you to lose your identity. Lost identity causes low self-esteem because if you don't know who you are others are able to decide who you are. Unfortunately many times they want to use your lack to their advantage so they give you a skewed image of yourself. You can spend many years of your life with a skewed image of who you are based upon the wrong words that someone used to describe you. This sounds ludicrous I know, but it's so true and happens all of the time. You become what they say you are and begin to transform yourself into that image. You don't believe me? Take a few minutes and think about what the people in your life say to you or about you? Are they correct in their assessment?

We've talked about who you say you are and how you'd like to be known let's take a look at who God says you are.

We will first examine who God is.

Exodus 3:13-15

¹³ Moses said to God, "Suppose I go to the Israelites and say to them, 'The God of your fathers has sent me to you,' and they ask me, 'What is his name?' Then what shall I tell them?"

¹⁴ God said to Moses, "I am who I am.[a] This is what you are to say to the Israelites: 'I am has sent me to you.'"

¹⁵ God also said to Moses, "Say to the Israelites, 'The Lord,[b] the God of your fathers—the God of Abraham, the God of Isaac and the God of Jacob—has sent me to you.' "This is my name forever, the name you shall call me from generation to generation.

There are three primary names of God: Elohim (God), Jehovah or Yahweh (Lord), and Adonai (Lord). Each of these names emphasizes a different nature of God. Elohim emphasizes God's strength and creative power. Yahweh expresses God's self-existence, particularly in relation to humanity and Adonai means master and underscores the authority of God. It's important that you realize that God has many different attributes. This means that one word does not define Him, he is multi-faceted. You, made in the image of God, are also multi-faceted. You are not one-dimensional; you were created for various purposes and are many different things. If you want to serve God better you need to know His attributes. Throughout the bible we see the many attributes of God at work.

In the beginning, we see the creative hand of God at work. Take a look at the sky, clouds, sun, moon, trees, lakes, stars. Really take a look at them... this is God's handiwork. The earth is really a beautiful place. Think about the seasons and how they are characterized....the beautiful powdery snow in the winter, blooming flowers in spring, green, lush grass in summer and panoramic color of leaves in the fall. It's amazing really. Don't forget the mountains, valleys, canyons, oceans...wow! What a creative God!!

Next take a look at yourself. You are created in God's image. Isn't that amazing? We are all so different with many diverse abilities and gifts but all created in the image and likeness of God. It is this image that makes us vitally important to God. That's why we must be careful what we reflect and who we connect with.

I always like to read different poems about God creating woman; they are so inspirational and really highlight the characteristics that are so much a part of who God is and wants to be to us if we allow Him to be. When I think of women reflecting God's image I always think of the other interpretation of El Shaddai which is God, the Breasted One or Many Breasted, because He is the Nourisher, Strength-giver, and so, in a secondary sense, the Satisfier, who pours himself into believing lives. As a fretful, unsatisfied babe is not only strengthened and nourished from the mother's breast, but also is quieted, rested, satisfied, so El Shaddai is that name of God which sets Him forth as the Strength-giver and Satisfier of His people.[6] When I first heard this interpretation of El Shaddai I thought it was strange; to think of the All Mighty and Powerful God as the Breasted One just didn't seem to fit but as a nourisher and strength giver I can find myself in Him because that's what I am as a woman. It's also what the Holy Spirit is in the believer's life; a Comforter.

Having a nourishing side does not take away from the authority of God. We see Him large and in charge throughout the Bible. We see him as destroyer and sustainer.

God is sovereign meaning He is the supreme ruler and has supreme power God is infinite meaning He is limitless; no end; extending indefinitely

God is immutable meaning He is unchangeable or unable to be changed

Read Job 38 and identify attributes of God.

In Chapters 38-41 God reminds Job of His sovereignty, His infiniteness, and His immutability.

Take time to read and really absorb chapters 38-41. God is driving home the point that He is God and that not only has He done all of these great and magnificent things but He also took care of every small detail. Rightfully so, Job is humbled and when we think of who God is we should be humbled also. We cannot begin to imagine the mind of God.

We have to recall what we have learned thus far; God did not create anything without a purpose so when we remember who God is it should help us to accept who we are.

Chapter 6

Learning To Value Myself

We did not explore fully who God is because it would take eternity to really know Him. Another reason that we didn't dig too deeply is because it's important that you establish a relationship with God for yourself. When you hear testimonies many times the person giving the testimony may say that God is their healer, lawyer, doctor, father, mother, and the list can be so long until you wonder what problems they can have if God is everything to them. Many of the people in the audience listening to the testimony may not know God as any of those things He may just be their friend so they can't really relate. You need to determine who God is to you. The only way that your relationship will grow is by allowing God into your life and recognizing His role in your life.

When I was first growing in Christ I learned that God is your father. I loved God but I had a really hard time with seeing Him as my father because I never had a father. I know that many of you are thinking that not having a father should have made it easy to accept God into that empty spot but just the opposite was true. I would hear ministers say just go to your Heavenly Father and tell Him what you want but I didn't know how to go to any father and tell him what I want, I just knew how to go out and get what I want. I wasn't taught to sit back and wait for anyone to do anything for me, definitely not a father because I would have been waiting forever. I also didn't know how to have a relationship with a father. I watched a couple of my girlfriends interact with their fathers and the relationship seemed so gentle, kind and submissive. My friends' fathers would be there to take care of little things for them, help them make decisions or just as support. I didn't know how to be a submissive daughter relying on her father. I never really saw a man do anything to care for the family. My first stepfather lived with us when I was almost 16 years old. He wasn't a biological father to me or my siblings and he wasn't trying to pretend to be. He had a son of his own from his first marriage and it was quite apparent that he knew how to be a father because when his son came to visit he would spend time with him and take time to talk to him. Of course, this caused a little resentment because we lived with him every day and he never took time to be fatherly with us or even take any interest in anything that we were doing.

There wasn't just a shortage of father's in my life but a shortage of males period. The women in my family were the breadwinners, and the movers and shakers. Growing up and seeing women do everything and the men being non-existent made it very hard to trust men, rely on men or even have much respect for men. These were issues I had to overcome to have a right relationship with Christ. I thank God for patience and grace because in time I overcame these things and could see God as my Father and see men correctly. Most importantly I saw myself correctly. Once you know who you are and understand that you were created with purpose everything else comes into alignment.

We've examined who we are based on self-identification and family identification now let's look at who we are based on God-identification.

³ When I consider your heavens, the work of your fingers, the moon and the stars, which you have set in place,

⁴ what is mankind that you are mindful of them, human beings that you care for them?[a]

⁵ You have made them[b] a little lower than the angels[c] and crowned them[d] with glory and honor.

⁶ You made them rulers over the works of your hands; you put everything under their[e] feet:

> ⁷ all flocks and herds, and the animals of the wild,
>
> ⁸ the birds in the sky, and the fish in the sea, all that swim the paths of the seas.
>
> (Psalm 8:4-9 NIV)

Man was created on the sixth day of Creation and is the grand climax of all that God created. Instead of allowing the waters and the earth to bring forth man as God did with the sea life, birds and animals, He said "Let us make man in our image, after our likeness:…" there was a hint of intimacy. God formed man Himself. Also after God formed man of the dust He breathed into his nostrils the breath of life. He was giving man His likeness (Spirit). Man was created especially for fellowship and communion with God. Man has great value to God, so much so that He sent His only begotten Son to restore man into fellowship and relationship with Him.

God values you so it is important that you value yourself as:

- Being Made in the Image and Likeness of God
- A Man
- A Member of the Body of Christ

You must understand that no matter what you have gone through you were not a mistake. God chose who you would be born to and the day and time that you would be born. Like He told Jeremiah in Jeremiah 1:4-5

> ⁴ Then the word of the Lord came unto me, saying,
>
> ⁵ Before I formed thee in the belly I knew thee; and before thou camest forth out of the womb I sanctified thee, and I ordained thee a prophet unto the nations.

God expects you to value yourself because you were created in His image.

Even after the fall we still maintain an image of God although it is a marred image. God's purpose is to conform us to the image of Christ.

You were predestined to be conformed to the image of Christ it is not by happenstance that you are still here or that you have been drawn by God's Spirit into a relationship with Him.

What does it mean to be made in the image of God? Having the "image" or "likeness" of God means, in the simplest terms, that we were made to resemble God. Adam did not resemble God in the sense of God's having flesh and blood. Scripture says that "God is spirit" and therefore exists without a body. However, Adam's body did mirror the life of God insofar as it was created in perfect health and was not subject to death.

The image of God refers to the immaterial part of man. It sets man apart from the animal world, fits him for the dominion God intended him to have over the earth and enables him to commune with his Maker. It is a likeness mentally, morally, and socially.

Mentally, man was created as a rational, volitional agent. In other words, man can reason and man can choose. This is a reflection of God's intellect and freedom. Anytime someone invents a machine, writes a book, paints a landscape, enjoys a symphony, calculates a sum, or names a pet, he or she is proclaiming the fact that we are made in God's image.

Morally, man was created in righteousness and perfect innocence, a reflection of God's holiness. God saw all He had made (mankind included) and called it "very good". Our conscience or "moral compass" is a vestige of that original state. Whenever someone writes a law, recoils from evil, praises good behavior, or feels guilty, he is confirming the fact that we are made in God's own image.

Socially, man was created for fellowship. This reflects God's triune nature and His love. In Eden, man's primary relationship was with God (implies fellowship with God), and God made the first woman because "it is not good for the man to be alone". Every time someone marries, makes a friend, hugs a child, or attends church, he is demonstrating the fact that we are made in the likeness of God.

Part of being made in God's image is that Adam had the capacity to make free choices. Although he was given a righteous nature, Adam made an evil choice to rebel against his Creator. In so doing, Adam marred the image of God within himself, and he passed that damaged likeness on to all his descendants. Today, we still bear the image of God, but we also bear the scars of sin. Mentally, morally, socially, and physically, we show the effects of sin. [7]

Man

God also expects you to value being a man. Throughout the bible male characteristics are attributed to God. Jesus was a man. He gave Man dominion over everything on the earth. Man is a ruler. Man is a leader. Man is the head. Everything that was made was made for man. James Brown was right in his song It's A Man's Man's World when he sang this is a man's world, (he was also right when he said it wouldn't be nothing without a woman or girl but I will give women their shout out later).

Raise your hand if you think the above statement is true.

I'm sure that most of you raised your hand because this is really not a mystery to anyone. You can just read the bible, look at history, look at the news; in some countries women still don't have the same rights as men. Even in the United States which is considered one of the most forward thinking and progressive countries in the world there are still disparities in pay between men and women.

So if it's all about the man, why do so many men have identity crises?

I'm not talking about the lack of role models in African American homes and communities, we've exhausted that angle I'm talking about the problem with all males regardless of race, economic status, and having or not having role models.

What has caused this identity crisis? In Chapter 5, Who Am I? we talked extensively about how your identity was formed, family identification and lost identity so you may feel like we've already covered this. In this area we will cover identity that makes you definable and recognizable as a man but most importantly we'll also look at those distinguishing characteristics of a man of God.

There are certain characteristics that are inherent to men. Let's look at physical characteristics.

We'll start by examining the animal kingdom. God created each animal with certain attributes that allows them to function and adapt to their environment; how they get food, how they eat, what alerts them to danger, how they defend themselves, raise and take care of their offspring and so many other things.

Take a look at the lion. I like to use the lion because he is also the king of his domain.

The lion is a member of the cat family, and shares many common traits of this family. The body is very muscular, with less bone mass than other animals of comparable size. This is also responsible for the grace of movement we associate with members of the cat family. The forebody of the lion is very powerfully built, and has the greatest forebody strength of any cat, except possibly the tiger. This enables the lion to deliver blows with its forepaws heavy enough to break a zebra's back. The bones of the front legs are twisted in such a manner as to give a great range of motion to the forelimb.

Each paw is equipped with soft pads to make its movements quiet. Like most carnivores, lions are digitigrades walkers. This means they essentially walk on their toes. But, the majority of the animal's weight is borne by the main paw pads, which would correspond on a human to the palm of the hand at the base of the fingers.

Extra bones in the toe joints give the toes a wide range of motion. The claws are retractable and very sharp.

The retractable feature helps keep the claws sharp, and prevents injury during play, etc. The dewclaw on the front limbs is often used as a toothpick. The claws grow as a series of layers. As a layer wears, it is shed, and anew sharp-pointed claw is exposed. The claw on a large lion can be 1 1/2 inches (38 mm) or more from base to tip along the curve.

The body is covered with a sandy brown coat in most subspecies of lions, but there is a white variant that shows up once in a while, especially in the Timbavati region of South Africa. (The white variant is also showing up more and more among captive lion populations.) Lions with a very dark brown coat have been observed, but this is quite rare. The coat color of a lion is not determined so much by the color of the hair, but by the ratio of light-colored hairs to dark-colored hairs

The mature male lion has a mane that covers the backside of the head, and the shoulders. The extent of the mane varies from individual to individual, with some having no mane at all, while others have a luxurious mane that runs onto the body, along the abdomen, and even onto the fronts of the back legs in exceptional specimens. The mane varies in color from the rest of the body, and tends to grow darker with age. Some lions in the Serengeti area and from North Africa have a nearly black mane. Just like the body hair, the mane color is determined by the ratio of dark hairs to light hairs present. The mane hair is stiff and wiry, like stiff horsehair. Besides its primary role of protecting the male during fights, it has been discovered that female lions prefer males with bigger and darker manes.

The eyes are proportionately larger than in other comparable-sized animals, and possess round pupils. Lions, like most cats, are visual animals. The eyes are also well-adapted for use under very low light. This helps the lion hunt at night. Contrary to popular notion, a lion's eyes do not glow in the dark, but they contain a special reflective coating that will reflect even moonlight. This coating increases the lion's visual acuity in very low light by ensuring that every possible photon of light makes it to the cells in the retina. Their eyes are effective even by starlight. A white circle just below the eyes helps reflect light into the eyes to further improve night vision. Like most mammals, lions have a nictitating membrane which serves to clean and protect the eye in some circumstances. Lions, like most cats, have limited ability to move their eyes side-to-side, and must turn the head to look in a different direction.

The sense of smell is well developed. Lions mark their territories by means of scent deposits, necessitating a good sense of smell. This also helps them find kills made by other predators, and perhaps obtain an easy meal by driving the other predator off their kill. Another interesting thing that lions and all other cats possess is a special olfactory organ on the roof of the mouth called a Jacobson's organ. Sometimes, you will see a lion, or even your cat, grimace when smelling something. They are opening their lips to draw air over their Jacobson's organs. This grimacing gesture is called Flehmen.

The sense of hearing is perhaps only slightly above average. The ears can be swiveled over a wide angle to enable the lion to hear distant sounds, and know what direction they are coming from.

The lion's tail is the only one in the cat family with a tassel at the tip. (Ligers also have a tassel, but they are not found in the wild.) This tassel conceals a spine, which is the last few tail bones fused together. What function this spine serves, if any, is unknown. The tail is very important for overall balance. Females also use their raised tail as a 'follow me' signal for the cubs. They also use it to signal each other during a group hunt.

The lion's teeth are well adapted for killing their prey and eating it. The great canine teeth are spaced such that they can slip between the cervical vertebrae of their favorite-sized prey animals, and sever the spinal cord. The shape of the back teeth, which are called carnassial instead of molars, makes them work like a pair of scissors, for cutting pieces of meat. The jaw is not capable of moving side-to-side, like ours. This helps keep the carnassial teeth in alignment for cutting. The rest of the teeth are conical, and designed for cutting and tearing. Lions, like all cats, do not chew their food, but swallow it in chunks. They also use only one side of their mouth at a time. This trait is also common to all cats, and is caused by the inability of the jaw to move side-to-side. The tongue is covered with rough spines, called papillae. This helps the lion scrape meat off of bones, and acts like a comb for grooming.

The digestive system of the lion is simple, not unlike a human's. Meat is fairly easy to digest, and the elaborate digestive mechanisms present in their prey for breaking down cellulose are not needed. Cats, in general have the shortest digestive tracts of all animals.

A lion's body temperature ranges from 100.5 to 102.5 degrees Fahrenheit. (38.05 - 39.16 degrees C.)

No physical description of the lion would be complete without some mention being made about its magnificent roar. Only four cats can roar: The lion, tiger, leopard, and jaguar. These four cats have been assigned to the genus Panthera because they can roar. Of these cats, the lion roars the most. It is believed the roar serves to alert other lions of an individual's presence. Roaring choruses of several lions, or a whole pride, also take place. When a lion roars, it can do so with enough force to raise a cloud of dust. Roaring is made possible by a special two-piece hyoid bone.

Here are a few physical characteristics that are inherent to men:

- Larger Adam's apple
- Stronger, more muscular bodies
- Larger bone structure
- Lower body fat
- Thicker skulls
- Thicker skin

As you can see there's a big difference between the lion's physical characteristics and a man's. This is because almost everything that an animal needs for survival is on or in its body while God made man with the capacity to be rational and to reason. Instead of having to use your body for everything you use your mental capacities as well; brain and brawn.

The reason that we talked about the lion is because when you see a lion you can easily identify that he is a lion; he looks and acts like a lion. There is no question that a lion is a lion. We talked about physical characteristics of a man but not every man has these characteristics, there are a lot of variations and conditions but for the most part, unless he's trying to fool you, when you see a man you are able to identify immediately that he is a man. What about a man of God? Is he easy to identify? I'm not talking about a priest or pastor with a collar or older pastors who for some reason are easily identifiable. I'm talking about a man that professes to love God. If that is you, your first label should be as a man of God. I'm not talking about a position but an identifier. Your life and character should proclaim that you are a man of God before you're identified as husband, father or CEO. That's why many men have an identity crisis; your mouth says one thing while your life shows another. What you say doesn't line up with how you are identified. One example I can give you of this is during the Grammys, Oscars or any awards show when different performers go up to receive their award the first shout out that they give is to God. This is normally pretty amazing when their body of work does not glorify God in any way. As a matter of fact it may even do just the opposite; lead people away from belief in God.

How are you identified? Are you having an identity crisis? Are you the guy at the work site that tells dirty jokes, hit on all of the women, and then talk about what the men's group at your church is doing? I am always amazed when men that flirt with me outrageously and inappropriately invite me to their church. Really! I'm not saying that you have to be perfect that's not the goal but something should line up in your life.

Who do you emulate? Who or what are you using to help create your identity? I laugh when I hear or see young preachers trying to emulate older preachers or famous preachers. If that works for them that's fine but remember it takes more than a certain inflection in your voice or delivery style. You have to be deliberate and ensure that who you represent to the world lines up with who you are claiming to be.

The bible is your best resource when forming your identity because it shows many men of God and how they pleased God and was in right relationship with Him. Jesus is our best example but we will also look at other men that God used:

David (King) Elijah (Prophet) Paul (Apostle)

David

If you have been in church for any length of time you have heard many sermons about David. Everything from killing Goliath to coveting and taking Bathsheba, to being pronounced dead when he was no longer interested in having a young woman in his bed. You can feel a lot of different emotions regarding David but one thing that can't be overlooked is that God considered him a man after His own heart.

> "And when he had removed him (Saul), he raised up unto them David to be their king; to whom also he gave their testimony, and said, I have found David the son of Jesse, a man after mine own heart, which shall fulfil all my will. Acts 13:22, parentheses mine

Why did God call David a man after His own heart? Pastor Ron Edmondson gives us insight into the character of David through his post, 10 Reasons David is A Man After God's Own Heart.[9] These are taken from David's psalms or songs:

Humble – *Lowborn men are but a breath, the highborn are but a lie; if weighed on a balance, they are nothing; together they are only a breath.* Psalm 62:9

Reverent – *I call to the Lord, who is worthy of praise, and I am saved from my enemies.* Psalm 18:3

Respectful – *Be merciful to me, O Lord, for I am in distress; my eyes grow weak with sorrow, my soul and my body with grief.* Psalm 31:9

Trusting - *The LORD is my light and my salvation— whom shall I fear? The LORD is the stronghold of my life— of whom shall I be afraid?* Psalm 27:1

Loving – *I love you, O Lord, my strength.* Psalm 18:1

Devoted – *You have filled my heart with greater joy than when their grain and new wine abound.* Psalm 4:7

Recognition – *I will praise you, O Lord, with all my heart; I will tell of all* your wonders. Psalm 9:1

Faithful – *Surely goodness and mercy will follow me all the days of my life, and I will dwell in the house of the LORD forever.* Psalm 23:6

Obedient - *Give me understanding, and I will keep your law and obey it with all my heart.* Psalm 119:34

Repentant - *For the sake of your name, O Lord, forgive my iniquity, though it is great.* Psalm 25:11

If you recall David did some foul things and made many mistakes, some that even got people killed. Yet he understood how to humble himself before a forgiving God and repent.

He exemplifies the type of man that God appoints as king and makes covenants that impact all of his generations after him.

Wouldn't you like to hear God say_(enter your name here) is a man after mine own heart and shall fulfill my will? If so, learn from David.

Elijah

- Elijah is known as being Israel's most famous prophet. What sets Elijah apart from other prophets of his day was:
- Great trust and loyalty towards God
- He is one who serves God; He stood before God
- He is a man of prayer; he combined the outward life of God's servant with the inner life of prayer
- He was a leader and was able to pass his mantle
- He did not die but was taken up into heaven in a whirlwind in a chariot of fire with horses of fire

Elijah exemplifies the kind of man that God wants to bring to greatness. Take time to read about Elijah starting in 1 Kings, chapter 17. Elijah is a mystery. When you are first introduced to Elijah half way through 1 Kings, you only find out where he's from nothing is related about his ancestry and then at the beginning of 2 Kings in chapter 2 he's basically taken up into heaven in a fiery chariot with fiery horses. Wow! In between you do see his genuine faith in God and although we see him bravely challenge the prophets of Baal, God also tells him to hide. If God has been using you mightily and openly and then all of a sudden you're called to a place of hiding or being out of the limelight, Elijah's story may be a revelation to you.

Paul

One word that can really sum up Paul is zealous. He had lots of zeal when he was persecuting Christians and after his conversion he had lots of zeal for Christ.

Chuck Swindoll writes a great book about the Apostle Paul called, Paul, A Man of Grace and Grit. What I like most is although Paul is considered one of the most influential people in the bible next to Jesus he is a lot like you and me. His life is a testament to how God can take someone who describes himself as chief among sinners and totally turn his life around. Paul was very open and honest about his failings, his weaknesses and his condition. He gives hope to all of us that no matter how far we have sank into depravity and sin if we are convicted of our sin and repent, God will forgive us and can drastically change our lives. There are many attributes about Paul that I can list but here are a few [10]:

- Persistence
- Patience
- Courageous
- Humble
- Uncompromising
- Yielding
- Ethical
- Forgiving

You can see Paul's attributes throughout Acts and in the letters that he wrote to the churches. Paul's writings are still relevant today and are a blue- print for living a Christian lifestyle for believers. Take time to read Acts and the 13 epistles penned by Paul. Also *Paul, A Man of Grit and*

Grace by Chuck Swindoll will be an interesting and enlightening read.

We have examined 3 men from the bible whose lives were pleasing to God. They were leaders, men of greatness, men with influence and men entrusted by God to advance His kingdom. These are the type of men that you want to emulate. The only way that you can emulate someone is by studying his life, actions, and motivations.

I encourage you to choose different identity traits from each and make them a part of your identity. Everything starts with knowing who you are and ensuring that what you do and say lines up with who you are.

Once you start to walk in your true identity every other area in your life will line up. You will be the husband, father and leader that you want to be. You will know how to love and lead your family; deal with your employees or co-workers; manage your resources and be a good steward over what God has blessed you with.

Are you the man that God has called to greatness?

Body of Christ

27 Now you are the body of Christ, and each one of you is a part of it.

12 Just as a body, though one, has many parts, but all its many parts form one body, so it is with Christ.

13 For we were all baptized by[a] one Spirit so as to form one body—whether Jews or Gentiles, slave or free—and we were all given the one Spirit to drink.

14 Even so the body is not made up of one part but of many.

15 Now if the foot should say, "Because I am not a hand, I do not belong to the to the body," it would not for that reason stop being part of the body.

16 And if the ear should say, "Because I am not an eye, I do not belong to the body," it would not for that reason stop being part of the body.

> 17 If the whole body were an eye, where would the sense of hearing be? If the whole body were an ear, where would the sense of smell be?
>
> 18 But in fact God has placed the parts in the body, every one of them, just as he wanted them to be.
>
> 19 If they were all one part, where would the body be?
>
> 20 As it is, there are many parts, but one body.
>
> 21 The eye cannot say to the hand, "I don't need you!" And the head cannot say to the feet, "I don't need you!"
>
> 22 On the contrary, those parts of the body that seem to be weaker are indispensable,
>
> 23 and the parts that we think are less honorable we treat with special honor. And the parts that are unpresentable are treated with special modesty,
>
> 24 while our presentable parts need no special treatment. But God has put the body together, giving greater honor to the parts that lacked it,
>
> 25 so that there should be no division in the body, but that its parts should have equal concern for each other.
>
> 26 If one part suffers, every part suffers with it; if one part is honored, every part rejoices with it.

1 Corinthians 12:12-27 sums up nicely the unity and diversity in the body of Christ. If you have accepted Christ as your savior you are a member of the body of Christ. For any church or ministry to function every member must do his or her part. As members it is important that you value your gifts and talents and use them to build the ministry and edify God. If jealousy or envy causes division in the body, the body will not function properly. See the examples in the scriptures above and also think about your own body. If one part doesn't work properly it affects every other area of the body and just because the parts are not seen or don't seem significant, they are. So it is with gifts. If you were not called

to be on a pulpit preaching, or singing or any gift that takes center stage it doesn't matter because what you do behind the scenes is just as important as what is done before the crowd. As a matter of fact without the behind the scene people the person taking center stage can't function as well. We all need each other. God created us for relationship and fellowship with Him and with each other. It is sad to see a large ministry with only a hand full of dedicated laborers. It's unfair to everyone when you don't use your gift. It's also a reproach to God to have gifted you and you do nothing with your gift but hide it like the man in the parable of the talents. Many times we wonder why our lives are not moving in the direction that we want it to go and why God is not answering our prayers. The answer is we do not have our priorities in order. We don't seek God first to know how He wants us to move. The second reason is that God does not trust us; we are not good stewards. If we are not using what He has already given to us why would He give us more?

> [16] A man's gift maketh room for him, and bringeth him before great men.

In Proverbs 18:16 it is the gift that opens doors for you and that brings you before great men or people of influence. God has already given you everything that you need to get everything that you need. All you need is to make Him your first priority, use the gift that He's given to you and walk in the purpose that you have been created for. It sounds very simple but it seems to be very hard to do because so many people struggle with this. I think that gifts is one area that the enemy uses to derail and distract us. Many times things that come easily or effortlessly to us are not as exciting and the enemy knows this so he opens us up to things that have absolutely nothing to do with using our gifts or walking in purpose. I listen to so many people that are excited and passionate about everything except the gift that God has placed in them. I can use my daughter as an example. Since she began to utter sounds she has been a singer. She could probably sing better than she could talk. When she sings for family and friends it brings them joy and peace. When she was a toddler she could sing Mariah Carey's songs and hit the high notes. She loves all music, from the Staple Singers to LeAnn Rimes. She can hear music, write songs and even notices different background sounds in music that I never hear. She can make a really bad singer sound good. It is quite obvious that this is her gift. It is also quite obvious that she is not interested in pursuing anything at all in music. The extent that she uses her gift is to give private concerts to me and my mother and recently she began to sing in the church choir. She, like so many other people, doesn't value her gift. It's not consciously done. We don't say "God I don't want this gift" but we don't do anything with it and the gift is what God has given us to glorify Him, edify the church and obtain favor with.

> 3 For by the grace given me I say to every one of you: Do not think of yourself more highly than you ought, but rather think of yourself with sober judgment, in accordance with the faith God has distributed to each of you.
>
> 4 For just as each of us has one body with many members, and these members do not all have the same function,
>
> 5 so in Christ we, though many, form one body, and each member belongs to all the others.
>
> 6 We have different gifts, according to the grace given to each of us. If your gift is prophesying, then prophesy in accordance with your faith;
>
> 7 if it is serving, then serve; if it is teaching, then teach;
>
> 8 if it is to encourage, then give encouragement; if it is giving, then give generously; if it is to lead, do it diligently; if it is to show mercy, do it cheerfully. **Romans 12:3-8**

I want you to pay close attention to the end of verse 3 "in accordance with the faith God has distributed to each of you." Paul puts this here to remind the believer to not overestimate himself and try to exercise a gift that God has not given or to underestimate himself and fail to exercise the gift that God has given. So walking in and exercising your gift is in accordance to the faith that you have. If you have a little faith you have to operate on a little level, if you have great faith you can operate on a greater level. It is only through a closer relationship with God that your faith will increase. As you go through different test and trials and experience God's grace, provision, and protection your faith will begin to grow.

Maybe your problem is not that you are interested in pursuing something else instead of operating in your gift. Your problem may be that you don't know what gift you have. Some gifts are easy to recognize…singing, preaching, writing…but others may not be as recognizable. As you can see in the scriptures above not all gifts are what you would traditionally think of as a gift….serving, encouraging, giving but they are because it takes a certain grace to do these things, not everyone can do it effectively. I can tell you to think about what you do well or what comes easily to you to determine what gifts you have. As a matter of fact, there is an exercise that follows this lesson that will allow you to do that but more importantly than that I want to encourage you to seek God for your gift. Many times your gift and purpose are tied together. When you began to seek the Kingdom of God and all its righteousness first this is a part of all "these things that shall be added unto you." I firmly believe that the best way to build your relationship with God is to go to Him with questions because God wants fellowship with you. If you draw nigh to God He will draw nigh to you. God does not want to keep things hidden from you. If he did why would the Holy Spirit have inspired so many men to write the bible?

Remember: God has already given you everything that you need to get everything that you need.

While we're on the subject of gifts there is one gift that we all have and that is to make disciples. This is our Great Commission. Christ would not have told us to do it if it wasn't in our capacity to do it. Matthew 28:18-20

[18] Then Jesus came to them and said, "All authority in heaven and on earth has been given to me.

19 Therefore go and make disciples of all nations, baptizing them in the name of the Father and of the Son and of the Holy Spirit,

20 and teaching them to obey everything I have commanded you. And surely I am with you always, to the very end of the age."

SHIFTING PARADIGMS FOR MEN

CHAPTER 7

Breaking Curses

In Chapter 3, *What Does God Say About Me*, we discussed The Fall and the curses that God pronounced on both the enemy and man. We are still living under these curses and it will not be until the resurrection that the curse will be lifted. These curses pronounced by God we can do nothing about but allow the Holy Spirit to give us comfort until our glorification. That is not the case with curses that have been passed from generation to generation. We can uproot those curses that have been a stronghold over our lives and continue to perpetuate themselves throughout generations of our families.

We examined how our history and past experiences affect our day to day lives. We talked about fears and other things that have been perpetuated in our families that hinder us or make us feel guilty about success. Before Christ came to fulfill the law, curses were passed from generation to generation; entire families were cursed because of the action of a few. In Numbers 16, Korath rebelled against Moses because he was upset that out of the Levites, Aaron and his sons were set aside as the priesthood. God opened up the earth and swallowed up everything that pertained to Korath; all his house, meaning wives and children, all 200 of the men that were with him and all of their goods. The same way that Korath's actions affected everything attached to him is how the actions of your past generations affect you and other members of your family. Think back to our past chapters and observations. We unearthed fears and norms that are still prevalent in our family today. We identified them, observed their affects in our families and in our lives but now it is time to go a little deeper and uproot some of these deeply rooted things that manifest as curses in our lives.

Many times these things are so deeply rooted and grounded in our lives and all of the lives that we have a front row seat in that it's hard to imagine a life without the dysfunction. Every man in your family has been a drunk for as far back as you can remember; your daddy was a drunk, your grandfather was a drunk, your grandfather's brother, Uncle Joe, was a drunk, even your favorite Uncle Arthur was a drunk. At every family function you knew they would be drunk and one of them just might make a scene. As a matter of fact it's expected and you, your siblings, and cousins only go because you know there's going to be drama. It's the same scene played out every year. The location may change, the weather may be different but no matter what the show will go on. This root has been allowed to grow stronger and stronger because no one has ever uprooted it. If you're not careful you may go out and be a drunk man too because that's what's normal to you.

Have you ever seen women that aren't satisfied in a relationship with a man unless there's some drama; he's either fighting with her or over her? That's because drama and chaos is normal to her. As a matter of fact her definition of love is spawned from this chaos. I've met women that don't believe a man loves her unless he's hitting her or arguing with her. I know this may sound strange to you but think about what "equals" love to you. Where did that come from? Does a woman giving you money or taking care of you "equal" love to you? Why? Where did that come from? Does a woman giving you lots of gifts "equal" love to you? Why? Does a woman being jealous and suspicious of other women and not wanting you to go out without her "equal" love to you? Why? What I'm getting at is there are some things that are so deeply rooted and grounded in you that it's causing curses in your life and you don't even realize it.

When I say curse I'm not talking about something a witch cast although the effects are the same. I'm talking about a loss of blessings, loss of satisfaction and ultimately loss of fulfilling your purpose. When God requires that we be holy that's a tall order. Apparently it's possible because God would not require something of us that is impossible to do but when we take that mandate seriously we realize that we have a lot of transforming to do. To determine what we will become we must first take a look at what we came from; our roots.

One of the meanings of the word root is the cause or origin of something. Isaiah prophesied that Christ would be a rod that comes forth from the root of Jesse. Basically the root is what anchors, supports or attaches something. If the root is unstable or not attached deep enough or isn't in a fertile environment whatever is attached to it will rot, be uprooted, and ultimately die. This process does not happen overnight, it may take many years because some things thrive in dark, dank, unfertile places for long periods of time.

In Matthew 13, *The Parable of the Sower*, Jesus gives an example of how having root produces fruit.

> 3 Then he told them many things in parables, saying: "A farmer went out to sow his seed.
>
> 4 As he was scattering the seed, some fell along the path, and the birds came and ate it up.
>
> 5 Some fell on rocky places, where it did not have much soil. It sprang up quickly, because the soil was shallow.
>
> 6 But when the sun came up, the plants were scorched, and they withered because they had no root.
>
> 7 Other seed fell among thorns, which grew up and choked the plants.
>
> 8 Still other seed fell on good soil, where it produced a crop—a hundred, sixty or thirty times what was sown.

When we talk about our roots we are talking about where we come from, and who we come from…what family, what background. It's very important that we understand our roots because it is the root that determines what fruit or outcome is produced and how that fruit or outcome is produced.

> 17 Likewise, every good tree bears good fruit, but a bad tree bears bad fruit.
>
> 18 A good tree cannot bear bad fruit, and a bad tree cannot bear good fruit.
>
> 19 Every tree that does not bear good fruit is cut down and thrown into the fire.
>
> 20 Thus, by their fruit you will recognize them.

Think about this in terms of a family tree. A seed is planted, primarily a man's sperm is planted into a woman that brings offspring. This offspring, or root grows. Even if the conditions are not the best, if the root stays in the ground and is not uprooted it will grow and inevitably branch out. The branches may not be the sturdiest, most stable or even have been rooted in the best soil but limbs will form. Some limbs will bud, bear leaves, some will break off. This is basically your family tree. You have the foundation, which is the common ancestor, the offspring of that ancestor and so forth and so on until it gets to you and your immediate family. When you read Old Testament books many times scripture traces the entire lineage of a family….this person begat that person and so forth. Also at the beginning of Old Testament books written by prophets, the author's parentage or lineage is described…the words of Nehemiah the son of Hachaliah; the vision of Isaiah son of Amoz. Isaiah even tells the prophecy of the lineage through which Jesus would come. So it's plain to see that there is significance in a family's lineage.

Your family tree is also the source of your bloodline. Blood is extremely important because God requires blood to cover sin. In Old Testament times the priest used the blood of animals to atone for the sins of the people; animals had to continually be sacrificed. When Christ came it was His blood shed once that became a propitiation for sin and that reconciles us to God. Outside of Christ your bloodline is cursed; it is exposed to sin without any way for redemption or justification.

When we are born, we are born naturally of blood and lineage but when we are born again or born of God we are born spiritually and supernaturally. The wine that we drink during communion represents the blood of Christ which is the new "blood" covenant that we are under today. This blood sustains our spiritual life because when we are to partake in communion, the body and the blood of Christ, we must first examine ourselves or our lives to ensure that we are worthy to partake.

Life is in the blood. Think about that for a second. Blood flows, when blood stops flowing it becomes clotted which can cause death. If we lose all of our blood, we will die. We received eternal life only through the shed blood of Jesus Christ. When God gave Moses the laws for the Israelites one of the laws was to not eat anything with the blood still left in it. That's because that meant it still had life in it. (This resulted in the Jews' kosher meat.) When Cain slew Abel, God asked Cain in Genesis 4:10,

> [10] The Lord said, "What have you done? Listen! Your brother's blood cries out to me from the ground.

The blood flows throughout your blood line and it carries nourishment and oxygen but also disease and sickness and things that we say are hereditary. In Chapter 2 when we talked about disobedience and the curses that come upon you from disobedience they fell into the following categories: internal calamities (death, despair, disease, and decline); external judgment (defeat before the enemy) and the transmission of judgment to your descendants. Jesus' disciples asked him in John 9, when he passed by a man which was blind from his birth, *"Master, who did sin, this man, or his parents, that he was born blind?"* They understood that curses were passed from generation to generation.

Disease and sickness are curses; mentally, emotionally or physically. Throughout the Old Testament when God pronounced a curse many times disease was a part of it. In Job we see that the enemy attacked him and caused all manner of evil to come upon him in all three of these areas, mentally by tormenting him with the thought that it was his fault these things befell him; emotionally by killing his children and servants; physically by bringing boils upon his body. Before accepting Christ these curses applied to us but once we accept Christ we are no longer under the curse. Galatians 3:13 tells us that "Christ has redeemed us from the curse of the law, being made a curse for us: for it is written, Cursed is everyone that hangeth on a tree".

So why are we afflicted with so many of the same sicknesses and diseases of our ancestors? The best answer that I can give for that is many times those curses were passed down to you before you accepted Christ. So by accepting Christ, the curses are broken but possibly the spirit or demon that had entered in before your conversion is still there. That's one of the reasons that the word admonishes us to be full of the Spirit so that there's no room for anything else. Although you have accepted Christ there are still spirits that had a legal right to you before your conversion, you have to cast those out and many of them may have come from sins of your ancestors. Think about your family tree. What internal calamities, external judgments or transmission of judgment is still operating today? Make a list of those things and confess them to God, declare those generational curses renounced and removed and cast out any demons associated with those curses. God has given us authority to cast out demons.

Sometimes we don't even realize it but we speak curses over our own lives.

5   Likewise, the tongue is a small part of the body, but it makes great boasts. Consider what a great forest is set on fire by a small spark.

6   The tongue also is a fire, a world of evil among the parts of the body. It corrupts the whole body, sets the whole course of one's life on fire, and is itself set on fire by hell.

7   All kinds of animals, birds, reptiles and sea creatures are being tamed and have been tamed by mankind,

> 8 but no human being can tame the tongue. It is a restless evil, full of deadly poison.
>
> 9 With the tongue we praise our Lord and Father, and with it we curse human beings, who have been made in God's likeness.
>
> 10 Out of the same mouth come praise and cursing. My brothers and sisters, this should not be. (James 3:5-10)

It is imperative that we watch what we say to others but it's also just as important to watch what we say to ourselves. Sometimes we pronounce judgment and curses over our lives, our children's lives and our whole family. Don't you know that the enemy walks to and fro seeking whom he may devour? Many times we give him all of the ammunition that he needs to devour us. You must speak life and not death. In past chapters we've talked about your identity and how it was shaped. We discovered that many times words shape who we become; words of love that bless you or words of hate or ignorance that curse you. My mother always spoke very positive things to me. The positive words that she spoke into my life built me up so much that no one can tear me down, not even her. I remember going through a very mouthy and sassy stage when I was around 13 years old and when I would get completely out of control my mother would call me a sassy sow (I grew up on a farm, so go figure). Well I knew what a sow was so when she'd call me that I'd say (to myself, I was not crazy) I'm not a sow, a sow is a hog and nothing about me is similar to a hog. What had happened is that my mom had told me who I was and had spoken so much positive into my life at such an early age that I rejected anything that didn't line up with that. Because of her words, I have been convinced my whole life that I can do whatever I set my mind to and that I'm destined for greatness.

What have you spoken into your life? What are you speaking now? What are you pronouncing over your home? Blessings or Curses?

Curses are evil or misfortune invoked upon someone and the result of the invocation. So think about the things that have been said about you or that you say about yourself that have actually come true. An example could be: I'm never going to get out of debt.

You must speak God's words over your life that is why you must read the bible; that is the only way that you will know God's words.

Remember: Out of the same mouth come blessings and curses.

If you have been pronouncing curses over your life or over other people's lives you need to put off the old man, repent, and spend more time being transformed by the renewing of your mind.

It's imperative before you move on to the next chapter that you make a break with the past. God won't do a new thing in you if you are still walking in the old things. Repent, forgive yourself, break the past's hold on your life, break curses and look forward. It's time to live in the present and prepare for the future.

Living for God has great benefits. If we really have faith, believe God's word, speak that word into and over our lives we will live a peaceful and abundant life. It can take you years to figure this out or you can decide to live this way now, the choice is yours. Let's see some of the benefits that come with serving our awesome God.

SHIFTING PARADIGMS FOR MEN

CHAPTER 8
Determining Who I Want To Be

The previous chapters have been retrospective. We've examined our past experiences, family history, and through deep introspection or self-examination our thinking, feelings and self-image. In this lesson we will talk about moving forward. To do this we must let go of the past; past hurts, disappointments, derailments, people, and things. By now you know what you must release and have either released those things or created a plan to release them. It is imperative that throughout the lessons that you were open and honest with yourself and really put in the work so that you are ready to move forward. You cannot take steps forward with the past weighing you down. You must shed those heavy death clothes, step out of those ashes and walk in the newness of life and stand fast in the liberty wherewith Christ has made you free, and be not entangled again with the yoke of bondage. We can't allow the past to determine our future because it either limits us and our propensity to walk into our purpose or it propels us to reach for too many things and our purpose is buried and neglected. You will never lead a fulfilling life if you do not operate in your purpose. You will always feel like something is missing or you will feel stagnant.

Take a moment and think about 10 people that are in your inner circle. How many of them do you think are living a fulfilled life? Why do you think they are? When you get an opportunity ask all 10 of them if they feel their lives are fulfilling. Some of the answers may surprise you. We are so good at hiding things and displaying an outward show of success when inside we feel so empty and unfulfilled. The people that always appear to have it together aren't always the ones that do; many times the people that seem disorganized with a lot of chaos may actually lead a more fulfilled life.

I won't assume that you aren't fulfilled or overlook the fact that you may already have your life planned out; your 5, 10 or 20 year plan may be already in place and working well but I challenge you to take a look at your plans and ensure that God is in the planning and that your purpose is being fulfilled.

I have always been a planner; I had 5 and 10 year goals and plans, I focused a lot of my energy on my goals and plans but I wasn't extremely obsessive; I allowed room for change because I like a little spontaneity too. For years my goals and plans fell into place exactly how I'd planned and expected. I ensured that prayer was a part of my plan and whenever God gave me a task I'd incorporate that into my plan also. I felt like I was on track to be and do exactly what would bring me success and check my purpose box too. In 2008, God began to speak to me about opening a company with my family. That wasn't a part of my plan. I had just retired from the Air Force in 2007, didn't have to work and was just traveling and enjoying life. Despite that, I was obedient to God and talked to my family about it. We decided to go for it and began to do the planning and research. Opening a business meant that I would have to move from Charleston, SC to Atlanta, GA because most of my family members were there. Although it wasn't a part of my plan it was doable; my husband was retired and waiting to go to Law School, my daughter was in a junior college at the time and was going to transfer back to a 4 year college soon anyway so moving wasn't that big of a deal, I also didn't really enjoy living in Charleston anyway. The biggest problem for me was moving from my house in Charleston to an apartment in Atlanta because I hadn't lived in an apartment in over 20 years.

We moved to Atlanta in August 2009 and started doing business in September 2009. Things were on an upward climb. We even opened a second business in June 2010. At the end of July 2010 everything crashed down around me; my marriage ended, my savings account had dwindled to nothing, my credit score had taken a nose dive, I didn't have any disposable income, I'd gone from abundant living to hand to mouth living. For the first time in my life, ALL of my plans had fallen apart. It's funny really because it reminded me of a cartoon I saw once, on the cartoon the narrator was saying that the man went down the drain and he literally went down a drain. That's how I felt, like my life literally fell apart; like I was split completely in two. It wasn't a gradual process it was quick and absolute. As a matter of fact, even new plans I made would fall apart. I felt numb and stagnant; I didn't know how to move forward without a plan.

This is when I decided to see a therapist. I was still angry over all of the lies and deceit and abuse and things had gotten even worse. I was angry and I knew that I would become viciously bitter if I didn't seek help. As I began to see my therapist we had to go backwards and come forward. Like we've done in this guide, we had to examine the past and determine what my values are and how different life experiences had affected my life, character, and outlook because ultimately these things affect why and how I make decisions. I learned a lot about myself, my relationships and how my childhood, my family values and norms had shaped me. I was able to see patterns that I never realized I had established and how again and again I'd end up at the same place. After each session I'd go home and think, rethink, analyze, and reanalyze everything that we'd talked about. I was able to see so many areas in my life that had been affected by my dysfunctional living and thinking. I didn't think it was dysfunctional when I was doing it but when I look back on it now I realize that it was totally dysfunctional. If I kept doing the same things and getting the same results or even doing what I thought were different things and getting the same results something was wrong and it most definitely was not "functioning" or working for me.

I began to work on those areas that I saw were causing me the most problems and pain. Many of them I was able to fix quickly by either inviting someone out of my life or inviting someone in. Some of them are still a work in progress but I work on them daily. I don't work on them alone because I can't fix all of my problems, I take them to God. The Bible tells me to "cast my cares on Him for He cares for me" and that's what I do. That's what God expects you to do also. He doesn't expect you to constantly be pulled back into situations in your past and get distracted or derailed. He expects you to release those cares to Him so that you can take care of His things and move forward. Luke reminds us in Chapter 9:62 that Jesus said "No man, having put his hand to the plough, and looking back, is fit for the kingdom of God."

I had to learn to live differently; God's plans became my plans. Even today I am still in learning mode. I'm learning to move when He says move, where He says move, how He says move. It is not easy; it requires complete trust and faith in God and His plan for my life; even on those days when I don't hear His voice or really know what direction to go in. I don't always succeed at this. Sometimes I miss Him and I go in the wrong direction and do what's comfortable to me but I must confess that those plans fall apart too. I'm finally at a point where I don't worry about what will happen anymore, God is in control. I just take each day as it comes; that doesn't mean that I don't play an active role in my destiny and purpose I'm just not the captain of the ship because I don't know what course to set sail on. My desire is Philippians 3:10-14:

[10] I want to know Christ—yes, to know the power of his resurrection and participation in his sufferings, becoming like him in his death,

[11] and so, somehow, attaining to the resurrection from the dead.

[12] Not that I have already obtained all this, or have already arrived at my goal, but I press on to take hold of that for which Christ Jesus took hold of me.

[13] Brothers and sisters, I do not consider myself yet to have taken hold of it. But one thing I do: Forgetting what is behind and straining toward what is ahead,

[14] I press on toward the goal to win the prize for which God has called me heavenward in Christ Jesus.

Paul lets us know in the above scripture that to know Christ, which should be every believer's desire, we have to "forget those things that are behind and press forward to the mark of the high calling in Christ Jesus." Whenever I find myself longing for the past life that I had I have to remind myself that God called me to now and that I must focus on now. If we are so busy allowing our past to hold us back how will we be able to know Christ or grasp the power of Christ's resurrection or participate in his sufferings. We will be too busy allowing our own suffering to overtake us and our suffering is in vain if it is not for righteousness sake. Many of us know and cite a lot of scripture but we must allow scripture to be illuminated for us so that we understand how to use it for our day to day lives. When we are in Christ we are freed from sin. Our old man is crucified that the body of sin might be destroyed, we should not serve sin. Nor should we be so guilty about the past that it hinders us from pressing forward into the future and toward the goal to win the prize or high calling of God. This will not be easy but it's necessary.

In the 13th verse Paul writes, "Forgetting what is behind and straining toward what is ahead", when you think of someone straining it brings to mind someone stretching or exerting themselves to the utmost; striving for something. Normally that takes a lot of effort, possibly even pulling against or away from something that has a hold on you like your past, people, or sin. In the 14th verse Paul writes "I press" when you think of pressing it is not a simple process it usually means that you're pushing against something. In this case it is you that you are pushing against; your past, experiences, desires, goals, plans, successes, defeats. So straining toward and pressing on sounds like being in a tug of war. That is exactly what it is. A tug of war between the old you and the new you. The old you that wants to wallow in the familiar: sin, self-pity, hurts and disappointments and the new you that wants a change: righteousness, peace, joy, and purpose.

Let's examine areas that will propel us into looking towards our future. In the previous lessons we've taken time to bury the dead things that so easily beset us so we now must look forward and springboard into the future that God has predestined for us.

First Things First

There are 5 truths that we must take into consideration when looking to the future.

- We no longer live for ourselves but for Christ
- We are a new creature
- It is our responsibility to be transformed
- We have a responsibility to others
- God has a plan for our lives

The realization of these 5 truths help us to establish a strong foundation that will root and ground us in who we are in Christ.

Living For Christ

> 14 For Christ's love compels us, because we are convinced that one died for all, therefore all died.
>
> 15 And he died for all, that those who live should no longer live for themselves but for him who died for them and was raised again.
>
> 16 So from now on we regard no one from a worldly point of view. Though we once regarded Christ in this way, we do so no longer.
>
> 17 Therefore, if anyone is in Christ, that person is a new creation: The old has gone, the new is here!

These scriptures from 2 Corinthians, chapter 5:14-17 puts things into perspective for us. As a matter of fact we are allowed to reinvent ourselves and verse 15 gives us the impetus for the change "And he died for all, that those who live should no longer live for themselves but for him who died for them and was raised again." That's amazing we are no longer living for ourselves but for Christ. It is Christ's love for us that compels us to live for Him. Compel means to force (someone) to do something; to cause (something) to happen by force; to drive or urge forcefully or irresistibly; to cause to do or occur by overwhelming pressure. So in essence God's love for us by sending Christ to die for our sins is so great that it forces us, drives or urges us and overwhelmingly pressures us to no longer live for ourselves but to live for Him. If you ever wondered how important love is to God or questioned the power of love, here is your answer. Christ has already epitomized this love for us by dying for all; He kept His end of the bargain so we are obligated by that love to meet our end of the bargain, which is to live for Christ.

So what does living for Christ mean? It means living a righteous life; being freed from sin we became servants of righteousness. We are God's special people: a chosen generation, royal priesthood, holy nation and peculiar people, why? That we would show forth the praises of him who hath called us out of darkness into his marvelous light. We show forth these praises through sacrifice, holy living, interceding on behalf of others and through love. Whereas in the Old Testament, Aaron's family was the priesthood, every believer is now the priesthood. So as the priest in the Old Testament sacrificed we are called to sacrifice: our bodies, our praise, our substance and our service. We are called to separate ourselves from actions, influences or people that will contaminate us and we are called to pray on behalf of our brothers and sisters in Christ and to love one another. This is possible if we do as verse 16 encourages and no longer regard anyone from a worldly (or fleshly) view. In Christ, you are spiritual so let the Holy Spirit be your lens.

There are too many scriptures in the bible that outline how we should live to put them all here. Take the time to read 1 Peter; 2 Corinthians 6:11-18; Romans 12:10-21; Romans 13:8-14.

Salt and Light

We also must remember that when we say we are in Christ we are not just representing ourselves and walking after our desires any longer. We are now representing Christ and the Body with all its members. We are responsible to unbelievers and a dying world. We are to be the salt of the earth meaning we must make a difference in the world. Salt is used to preserve food, melt coldness and heal wounds. This is a description of the believer in his relationship with the world around him, preserving the earth by slowing the decay of morals in society, healing the broken hearted, hurt and wounded.

What did Jesus mean by saying that salt which loses its savor is only fit to be walked upon? We know that Sodium Chloride will always taste the same as long as it remains chemically unchanged or pure. In a pure state, the mineral fulfills its primary purpose for existing. In Jesus' time, houses in Jerusalem often had an upper room for guests or other special occasions. The floors of these rooms were made of wood overlaid with plaster. However, ordinary wall plaster was too soft to be walked upon without cracking and crumbling. The addition of salt to the plaster made it hard enough to use for floors. Its mixing with plaster, however, makes it impure and unable to fulfill its role as a seasoning agent. In such an irreversible state it is only good to be walked upon. Christians, like salt, need to be pure in order to fulfill their purpose. [11]

We are also called to be the light of the world. We have a mission to the world. In our last lesson we talked about the Great Commission- discipleship. We are to let our light shine before men so that they may see our good works and glorify our Father. This scripture has been used so much that it doesn't make the impact that it should. A little light dispels complete darkness. It can be completely dark but you can use the light from a small cell phone to completely break through the darkness. Think about that… do you know how powerful that means you are supposed to be? Collectively our lives should be so righteous and our love so strong that we compel people to come to Christ. We force them to want what we got. When was the last time anybody asked you about Christ or what church you attend? Do the people that you work with know that you have a relationship with Christ? Do you affect anything in your workplace or have you been too busy focusing on yourself and your issues? Do you walk in victory or are you weighed down with so many problems that many times you're the one being consoled? Are you open minded to everything and everyone's lifestyle so much that no one can tell what your true values are? Do you portray a live and let live attitude?

When I get on my daughter about certain things she will say "Mom can I live" I always think this is funny because my daughter is an adult that still lives at home, if she really wanted to live she would be in her own place so I wouldn't know what she's doing and not be able to comment. As followers of Christ, the answer that we should give to the question, "can I live" is no, not if it's outside of Christ. That should be our answer to a dying world. What's the point of having all of this power living in us and not do anything with it. We are called to be salt of the earth and light to the world, not salt only in your church or social circle or light only in your sorority or family but beyond. This seems like a huge undertaking but if you live for Christ and not for yourself you will be surprised at the large impact you can make.

Now that we've read through scriptures that outline ways that we can live for Christ and identified ways to incorporate them into our lives let's step back because it's important that you understand how you are able to begin your new life.

A New Creature

In verse 17 we get a clean slate to start this new life, "Therefore, if anyone is in Christ, that person is a new creation: the old has gone, the new is here! We have spent the past several weeks rehashing the old trying to learn from it so that we can move forward and we get to today's lesson and realize that the old has gone, the new is here! Not the old is going and the new is coming. If you are in Christ, meaning have accepted Christ as your savior you are a new creation, the old has gone, the new is here.

This is where many people get confused because they don't see or feel like they've changed physically, mentally or emotionally. Let's talk about what happens.

In the beginning God created......In the first book of the bible, the first chapter, first verse we see God in creation. James Weldon Johnson, an African American author, politician, diplomat, critic, journalist, poet, anthologist, educator, lawyer, songwriter, and early civil rights activist wrote a poem entitled The Creation. I love hearing this "sermon" especially with sound effects and performed by a man with a deep, booming voice. You can feel God's impact.

The Creation

James Weldon Johnson (1871–1938)

(A Negro Sermon)

AND God stepped out on space,

And He looked around and said,

"I'm lonely—

I'll make me a world."

And far as the eye of God could see—5

Darkness covered everything,

Blacker than a hundred midnights

Down in a cypress swamp.

Then God smiled,

And the light broke,—10

And the darkness rolled up on one side,

And the light stood shining on the other,

And God said, "That's good!"

Then God reached out and took the light in His hands,

And God rolled the light around in His hands—15

Until He made the sun;

And He set that sun a-blazing in the heavens.

And the light that was left from making the sun

God gathered it up in a shining ball

And flung it against the darkness,—20

Spangling the night with the moon and stars.

Then down between

The darkness and the light

He hurled the world;

And God said, "That's good!"—25

Then God himself stepped down—

And the sun was on His right hand,

And the moon was on His left;

The stars were clustered about His head,

And the earth was under His feet. —30

And God walked, and where He trod

His footsteps hollowed the valleys out

And bulged the mountains up.

Then He stopped and looked and saw

That the earth was hot and barren. —35

So God stepped over to the edge of the world

And He spat out the seven seas;

He batted His eyes, and the lightnings flashed;

He clapped His hands, and the thunders rolled;

And the waters above the earth came down, —40

The cooling waters came down.

Then the green grass sprouted,

And the little red flowers blossomed,

The pine tree pointed his finger to the sky,

And the oak spread out his arms, —45

The lakes cuddled down in the hollows of the ground,

And the rivers ran down to the sea;

And God smiled again,

And the rainbow appeared,

And curled itself around His shoulder. —50

Then God raised His arm and He waved His hand

Over the sea and over the land,

And He said, "Bring forth! Bring forth!"

And quicker than God could drop His hand.

Fishes and fowls —55

And beasts and birds

Swam the rivers and the seas,

Roamed the forests and the woods,

And split the air with their wings.

And God said, "That's good!" —60

Then God walked around,

And God looked around

On all that He had made.

He looked at His sun,

And He looked at His moon, —65

And He looked at His little stars;

He looked on His world

With all its living things,

And God said, "I'm lonely still."

Then God sat down —70

On the side of a hill where He could think;

By a deep, wide river He sat down;

With His head in His hands, God thought and thought,

Till He thought, "I'll make me a man!" —75

Up from the bed of the river

God scooped the clay;

And by the bank of the river

He kneeled Him down;

And there the great God Almighty—80

Who lit the sun and fixed it in the sky,

Who flung the stars to the most far corner of the night,

Who rounded the earth in the middle of His hand;

This Great God,

Like a mammy bending over her baby,—85

Kneeled down in the dust

Toiling over a lump of clay

Till He shaped it in His own image;

Then into it He blew the breath of life,

And man became a living soul. —90

Amen. Amen. [12]

God's crowning glory was creating man. As we discussed in earlier chapters, man was the climax of all that God had accomplished in Creation. When God created man He created him in His image after His likeness. Genesis 1:27, "So God created man in his own image; in the image of God created he him; male and female created he them". From this scripture we can ascertain two things, first, as discussed, God created man (human race) in His image and secondly that he created both male and female as one flesh, at the same time. Eve's physical body was not formed until later but she was created at the same time as Adam. Adam and Eve were creatures; a creature is something that was created. We are all creatures living in creation.

In Chapter 3, *What Does God Say About Me?*, we talked about The Fall and the marred image that we are left with. Let's take a moment and dig deeper into what it means to be a new creation.

When God created man in His image, some of the attributes that man shared with God was to have dominion, live forever, and be spiritual. When Adam succumbed to temptation and ate the fruit it was his own lust that led him: lust of the flesh, lust of the eye and the pride of life. Adam's disobedience resulted in the human race being plunged into sin; when he fell all mankind fell. Although still in the image of God, mankind no longer reflected God's likeness. We were born into Adam's sin of the flesh so we automatically walk after the flesh in the likeness of Adam. By looking at our world you can see that man no longer has dominion over creation, that's why there are so many catastrophic events; man does not live forever and on his own man is not led by the spirit. That is why there is such a struggle between two natures. Paul talks about the struggle between flesh and spirit extensively. Before we were saved, the blood of Jesus was not a propitiation, or covering, for our sins so when God looked at us He saw sin and death, we were outcast, not a part of the family of God and in darkness, completely unlike our Creator who is light and who calls us into light. To regain the likeness of our Father we must be transformed.

Jesus tells the woman at the well in John 4:24, God is a Spirit: and they that worship him must worship him in spirit and in truth. The breath of life that God blew into Adam's nostrils at creation was to be Adam's life source and inner guide. We are only able to be spiritual and walk in truth when we are led by the spirit. Jesus told His disciples in John 16:13, "Howbeit when he, the Spirit of truth, is come, he will guide you into all truth; for he shall not speak of himself; but whatsoever he shall hear, that shall he speak: and he will show you things to come." Jesus is telling them that the Holy Spirit will lead them into truth or in this case the word truth can also mean fidelity which is the quality of being faithful or loyal and also the degree to which something matches or copies something else. These are the effects of the indwelling of the Holy Spirit; helping us understand the truth of the sacrifice of Jesus; God's work and word so that we can be faithful and loyal and transforming us into the likeness of Jesus so we can be accepted by the Father.

It is very important to understand the importance of the Holy Spirit dwelling inside of the believer and His role in the believer's conversion and transformation. At conversion a couple of things happen: you accept Christ's blood to cover your sins, you are adopted into the family of God, you are a member of the body of Christ and you accept the indwelling of the Holy Spirit. Ephesians 1:13-14 tells us:

> 13 And you also were included in Christ when you heard the message of truth, the gospel of your salvation. When you believed, you were marked in him with a seal, the promised Holy Spirit,
>
> 14 who is a deposit guaranteeing our inheritance until the redemption of those who are God's possession—to the praise of his glory.

When I first began ministering, I taught a series on the Holy Spirit. It was quite amazing because the Holy Spirit actually taught me about Himself. Many of the things that He taught me were in complete contradiction to what I had learned for years in church. It was very challenging because I had to shift my paradigm and be able to convey these revelations to my class. I learned a lot about the Holy Spirit and my thinking was changed in a lot of ways but what I still didn't grasp or could wrap my head around is that you didn't have to pray and ask God to baptize you with the Holy Spirit that it happens when you believe. That sounded too simple because years before at my home church I had to go through a complete ceremony to receive the baptism of the Holy Spirit with the evidence of speaking in tongues. It was a lengthy process. So, sticking to tradition, to close out the series I was teaching on the Holy Spirit, I did a week long prayer session for anyone that wanted to receive the baptism of the Holy Spirit. Several members came out and we would pray and basically beg God to baptize them with the Holy Spirit and give them the evidence of speaking in tongues. We did this for 5 days and not one person got baptized with the Spirit. We had a lot of great praise and worship and many people had testimonies that their prayer lives had changed dramatically but not one person was baptized with the Spirit. I was very discouraged and couldn't understand why God would not give His people the Holy Spirit if they wanted it so badly. It wasn't until a month or so later after I'd stopped being upset about the situation that the Holy Spirit began to teach me again about Himself. This time I was more accepting and completely let go of tradition and began to accept and walk in the truth.

What I missed is that those members had been sealed with the Holy Spirit when they believed. They didn't need more of the Holy Spirit, the Holy Spirit needed more of them. He was there waiting for them to acknowledge Him in their lives. I was able to look back on that week long prayer session and realize that many of them had received everything that they needed because they actually started to pray and began to incorporate prayer into their daily lives. We must be careful to remember that we were sealed with the Holy Spirit when we believed and will be sealed until the day of redemption. Something that's sealed is fastened or closed tightly. Think of sealing a letter or box. You don't want it to open when going through the postal channels so you ensure that the tape is strong enough and that every opening is sealed. Also when you seal something you only want it to be opened by the person that you are sending it to. This is how we are sealed by the Holy Spirit. All powerful God sealed us so even Hercules couldn't break that seal and the seal will be broken only by God when we are redeemed. This understanding should cause the believer to be mindful of the type of life he leads because the Holy Spirit lives inside of him. In Ephesians 4:17-32, Paul tells the Ephesians how to be a new creature in Christ.

17   So I tell you this, and insist on it in the Lord, that you must no longer live as the Gentiles do, in the futility of their thinking.

18   They are darkened in their understanding and separated from the life of God because of the ignorance that is in them due to the hardening of their hearts.

19   Having lost all sensitivity, they have given themselves over to sensuality so as to indulge in every kind of impurity, and they are full of greed.

20   That, however, is not the way of life you learned

21   when you heard about Christ and were taught in him in accordance with the truth that is in Jesus.

22   You were taught, with regard to your former way of life, to put off your old self, which is being corrupted by its deceitful desires;

23   to be made new in the attitude of your minds;

24   and to put on the new self, created to be like God in true righteousness and holiness.

25   Therefore each of you must put off falsehood and speak truthfully to your neighbor, for we are all members of one body.

26   "In your anger do not sin": Do not let the sun go down while you are still angry,

27   and do not give the devil a foothold.

28   Anyone who has been stealing must steal no longer, but must work,

> doing something useful with their own hands, that they may have something to share with those in need.
>
> ²⁹ Do not let any unwholesome talk come out of your mouths, but only what is helpful for building others up according to their needs, that it may benefit those who listen.
>
> ³⁰ And do not grieve the Holy Spirit of God, with whom you were sealed for the day of redemption.
>
> ³¹ Get rid of all bitterness, rage and anger, brawling and slander, along with every form of malice.
>
> ³² Be kind and compassionate to one another, forgiving each other, just as in Christ God forgave you.

Look at verse 30: "And do not grieve the Holy Spirit of God, with whom you were sealed for the day of redemption." Remember the Holy Spirit is a part of the trinity (Father, Son and Holy Spirit), when God said "Let us make man in our image and after our likeness" He was talking to Jesus and the Holy Spirit. Remember when we talked about losing the likeness of God before through Adam well when we accepted Christ the likeness of God came to live inside of us. That is why we are a new creature and that is also why we must walk as a new creature otherwise we are grieving the Holy Spirit.

Being a new creature means crucifying the flesh so that you can have more of the spirit. Ephesians 5:18, admonishes us to be not drunk with wine but be filled with the Spirit. When people are drunk they are considered under the influence of whatever was drank. It influences their speech, the way they walk, the way they see things and their actions. This is the influence that the Holy Spirit should have in a believer's life. The Holy Spirit is the first assurance that we are a new creature. Our seal indicates ownership, that we are genuine, and that we are preserved and kept safe. We no longer have to try to figure things out alone, we have the divine spirit living inside of us that tells us what God says concerning us and prays to God on our behalf, making intercession for us according to the will of God. You can't ask for more help than that. If you allow Him to, the Holy Spirit will lead you into your purpose. He will tell you what route to take, what to choose and what to reject.

Jesus called the Holy Spirit the comforter. He gives comfort to believers by: reminding them that they have been adopted into the family of God and are sons and joint heirs with Christ, no longer outcast; teaching them about God and the redemptive work through Jesus; being with them and helping them to transform so that they will have the likeness of God; and illuminating God's word so that they can live a victorious life.

God did not make us zombies or puppets that must do exactly what He says He gives us free will to choose who we will serve and how we will live so the Holy Spirit does not force you to allow Him to lead you into truth it's up to you to decide to be full of the Spirit and to submit your will. God is Alpha and Omega, the beginning and the end. He already knows your destination before you begin the journey, he predestined that but what happens along the road as you travel towards your destination lies in your hands.

Your Responsibility

1. Therefore, I urge you, brothers and sisters, in view of God's mercy, to offer your bodies as a living sacrifice, holy and pleasing to God—this is your true and proper worship

2. Do not conform to the pattern of this world, but be transformed by the renewing of your mind. Then you will be able to test and approve what God's will is—his good, pleasing and perfect will.

When you begin to study the bible to find out how to live as a Christian you quickly realize that it requires work on your part. The responsibility for your transformation lands flatly on your shoulders. You see passages that contain... you present, you put on, you be transformed, separate yourselves, try me, stand boldly, submit yourselves...I can fill this entire book with passages that put control back in your court. There can be no doubt that you will work out your own salvation many times with fear and trembling. After reading these passages, the believer may feel like he is fighting a losing battle. I've heard believers say that it's too hard to live for God. I would be lying if I said that I have never felt this way too. When you sit and listen to sermons and compare them to your lifestyle or you read the bible you can get overwhelmed and feel like there's no way you can do it. You think "with my issues and my way of thinking and past experiences I just can't win." When I feel this way I remind myself that I have already won. I already have the victory, my destination is already set I'm just trying to make the journey more enjoyable.

Being transformed and being holy is a lifelong journey. You will work on it every day of your life. When you don't get it right, you get another chance. What's that saying, if at first you don't succeed, try and try again? You get to try and try again. You are able to repent and start with a clean slate. You have the Holy Spirit living inside of you and He knows what it takes to make your journey more enjoyable and how to become the best you that you can be. What you have to do is wake up every day and commit to trying. You can't give up.

When I hear believers say "God knows my heart", many times this is when they are doing something totally contrary to the Word of God, my response to them is "Yes God does know your heart but He also understands the imaginations of your thoughts and He sees your actions." I'm not trying to be smug or judgmental I'm just being honest. What I hear when someone says God knows my heart is I'm not willing to put in the work to be transformed or to live holy so when I fall short I will use God's mercy as a scapegoat. The sad part about this is that this believer has stopped trying.

He's thrown in the towel. I don't omit myself from this. There have been times when I have pondered wrong, knowing it was not the best choice for me but did it anyway and said well God knows my heart. Once I'd take that attitude, getting back on track was always a little bit harder each time. When you make excuses for your behavior eventually you become desensitized. What helped me was I finally began to think about the Holy Spirit living inside of me unwillingly taking part in the wrong that I was doing. I may have exaggerated it because I'm kind of dramatic but I'd think of Him screaming inside of me. In my mind I was grieving Him horribly, He was there to help me turn away from wrong and to live more victoriously and I was mistreating Him. I'm not so quick to willingly and willfully do wrong now because that image so quickly convicts me.

Although a lot of responsibility for Christian living falls on your shoulders, you are not alone. Not only do you have the Holy Spirit but you also have the Word of God. The word gives you a formula for holy living. I don't think there's one particular formula but I think that the word can be made alive in your life in such a way that it makes it easier to live holy and be transformed. The first thing that you must realize is that this salvation walk is personal. Your walk may be totally different from your sister's, best friend's and from your parents. You may grasp and "put on" some things easier than others. You may be able to submit in some areas and have a hard time submitting in others. There's no right way to do it. Just like not everyone's journey is the same even if their final destinations are the same. Some may take an airplane, some may drive, some may take a train, some may have a smooth trip with no bumps, some may hit potholes along the road, some may even be stalled and have to postpone their trip while they work out issues but eventually all will arrive at the same destination. I will share my personal formula with you. It changes depending on what I'm facing but this is my basic foundation.

Matthew 6:31-34 starts my day, particularly verses 33 and 34.

[31] So do not worry, saying, 'What shall we eat?' or 'What shall we drink?' or 'What shall we wear?'

[32] For the pagans run after all these things, and your heavenly Father knows that you need them.

> ³³ But seek first his kingdom and his righteousness, and all these things will be given to you as well.
>
> ³⁴ Therefore do not worry about tomorrow, for tomorrow will worry about itself. Each day has enough trouble of its own.

I start my day seeking God. I praise Him and then I ask about His will for my life and to order my steps. When I start each day spending time with God, making Him my priority, everything falls into perspective for me. That doesn't mean I don't have challenges throughout the day but I feel that my steps are ordered so whatever I'm going through is just another step in fulfilling my purpose and towards my destination. I allow God to be concerned about my provision so that I can focus on what I must do for God. I am at peace which is so important to be able to accomplish all that is set before me in a day.

Next, James 4:7-8

> ⁷ Submit yourselves, then, to God. Resist the devil, and he will flee from you.
>
> ⁸ Come near to God and he will come near to you. Wash your hands, you sinners, and purify your hearts, you double-minded.

I daily submit every area of my life to God; my health, relationships, businesses, ministry. While submitting to God, I stand against Satan. The same way that Satan tried to tempt Jesus in the wilderness he will try to tempt you daily. I follow Jesus' example and use the Word so I won't fall into temptation but resist the devil. It's easy to do this when you know God's word so it's important that you study the word. If you don't know God's word you can be tricked and deceived just like Eve in the garden. Seeking God is my way of drawing near to Him. I treat Him the way I'd want to be treated by acknowledging Him and His importance in my life. We all want that in all of our relationships, particularly our close relationships why not give that in return especially to a God that gives so much to us and has given so much for us.

Repentance is also importance. Even if I may not remember any sins I committed, I may have omitted to do something that God called me to do so I repent daily. I don't want anything to stand in the way of my relationship with my Savior.

> 7 Dear friends, let us love one another, for love comes from God. Everyone who loves has been born of God and knows God.

Every day I ask God to help me love as He loves. This helps me get through the day without pulling anyone over a counter and choking them or ramming my truck into a car that cuts me off. Love helps me to be patient and tolerant. Love also helps me be at peace. It's an amazing feeling to go through the day at peace and not reacting to everything and everyone else's emotions.

The scriptures that I shared are foundational for me. Of course I meditate on many other scriptures depending on what I am dealing with throughout the day. I encourage myself, speak to situations, and encourage others among lots of other things. I believe that the bible is the infallible word of God and that it is a blueprint for life, my life, every day and every situation. I believe that the Word of God is alive and that life and death lies in the power of my tongue. If I am responsible for being holy and being transformed that means I am in control of everything: my words, my thoughts and my actions. I determine how effective the Holy Spirit and God's Word will be in my life. I determine how enjoyable my journey will be.

We have a responsibility to others

We've talked a lot about ourselves, our needs, desires, thoughts, and feelings but we must also think of others. When you come into relationship with Christ, you are a part of the body of Christ and as we discussed before it's made up of many members that actually rely on each other for the body to be functional and whole. We are called to love one another and not only those that are like minded but also to love our enemies. As God's example shows us, love is active. It is not lazy or remiss. We not only have a responsibility for ourselves but we are responsible for other believers and responsible to the lost.

Constantly throughout scripture we are encouraged to take care of other believers and pray for, feed and give drink to those that are considered our enemies. We are to freely give, bear the infirmities of the weak, meet the needs of the saints, rejoice with each other, weep with each other, edify each other, don't offend or condemn each other. I don't think that believers have a problem helping other believers through giving. I am still amazed at all of the volunteering, assistance, money that was raised, houses bought and communities built to help Hurricane Katrina survivors. There are many church missions that reach out to villages in Africa, Haiti and other countries that have a need. We freely give our money and time it's our attitudes and actions towards each other that could use shifting.

I talk to many people that don't go to church or left their old church because they had gotten hurt or were offended. I would always remind them that the church is full of hurting, broken people and that their expectations are too high. I don't say that anymore because although it is true that the church has broken and hurting people there should be an expectation of difference from the world's way of dealing with and interacting with each other. We should be setting the standard not falling below it. I always think about that song that says, *"please be patient with me God is not through with me yet, when God gets through with me I shall come forth as pure gold"* actually when God gets through you will not come forth as pure gold you will be placed in a box and lowered into the earth. While there is breath in your body, you will always be pressing towards the mark of the high calling in Christ Jesus. You will always need help in some area and be working on getting better. I'm not saying this to discourage you it's just the truth. God knows this but He still tells you to be transformed, to be holy, give, to cast out devils, to heal the sick, to raise the dead, to feed the hungry, minister to others and to love. Believers should always be pressing forward, building their faith, praying more, praising and worshipping more, getting stronger in their walk, maturing and looking more and more like Jesus. God has given you everything that you need to live victoriously and do His will.

There are no excuses.

We are sent to the lost. As we discussed earlier we are to be the salt and the light. Our mission is to tell unbelievers about the Good News of Jesus Christ. When I was young Jehovah's Witness would come to the door. Most people would either not open the door or open the door, take the pamphlet but not engage them. When they came to our house my grandmother and mother would invite them in and talk about God. They were not worried about the differences in their beliefs or about being converted to Jehovah's Witness because they were firm in their relationships with God but they could find commonalities with them. When I became an adult and they would visit my house, I would also let them in. When I really thought about it what Jehovah's Witness are doing is what we are all supposed to do; try to win lost souls. We are supposed to be telling unbelievers about our Lord and Savior Jesus Christ and His redemptive work on the cross. That doesn't mean that we have to go door to door to do this, there are many methods and platforms that we can use.

My mother always tells people about God. I jokingly say if you let her get a toe in the door she will kick the door in and walk on in. She is not ashamed of the gospel of Jesus Christ. As a matter of fact she is excited about talking to others about how good God is and makes every opportunity to witness. It doesn't matter where she is her light shines, the glory of the Lord draws the people, they began to talk to her and she tells them about God. I think that because she desires to witness about the goodness of the Lord, God gives her many opportunities. The excuse that many people use for not witnessing to others is that they don't know what to say. I believe that the only reason that you can't tell others about the goodness of the Lord is because you are not recognizing God's impact in your life. It doesn't take fancy words or in-depth knowledge of the bible to tell someone about what God has done for you. You don't have to have a title or be in a pulpit to minister to others. I think that too many times we assign ministry to those with titles and think that we are off the hook. Remember our great commission.

Despite how you feel about witnessing to others, God requires it of us all. If you just try, the Holy Spirit will help you. You don't have to be eloquent. Look at Moses, he didn't feel capable enough to go to Pharaoh and speak on behalf of God.

> 10 Moses said to the Lord, "Pardon your servant, Lord. I have never been eloquent, neither in the past nor since you have spoken to your servant. I am slow of speech and tongue."
>
> 11 The Lord said to him, "Who gave human beings their mouths? Who makes them deaf or mute? Who gives them sight or makes them blind? Is it not I, the Lord?
>
> 12 Now go; I will help you speak and will teach you what to say."
>
> **Exodus 4:10-12**

This is the same question that I ask you. Who gave human beings their mouths, is it not the Lord? Moses didn't even have the Holy Spirit living inside of him and you do. Do you think that any prophet in the bible wanted to go or felt confident enough to go and tell people that were deep in sin that they needed to turn from their wicked ways and serve God? No, they did not; Jonah tried to run away, Elijah hid in a cave, Jeremiah was forbidden to marry. Life for them was not easy because the people were angry with the prophecies that they proclaimed. They were threatened, beaten, sawn in two, beheaded and suffered many tragedies. Think about that. With all that they had to deal with they should have been afraid to witness and prophesy but that was their purpose and they walked in it. Are you walking in your purpose? Are you fulfilling the great commission? What are you afraid of? Why don't you witness to others?

I believe that Christians are the least radical group when it comes to displaying or proclaiming their faith. We are closet believers. When you look at other groups they are much more willing to tell others and sacrifice for what they believe. I don't agree with all of their methods and some of them are entirely too radical but the point that I'm making is that they are serious and committed to their beliefs and don't mind others knowing in what or whom they believe. The Christian community in the United States does not stand out as much. We come across as the true peace makers, we don't want to rock any boats. We accept anything as long as it doesn't interfere with our lives; we seem to have a live and let live attitude. I'm not saying that this is the sentiment but our actions or inaction make it look that way.

The Christian church looks like the world; there's not much of a distinction. I understand that we want to draw the world in but it's important that we don't let the world draw us in and that's what I see. The music, songs, dress, and ceremonies are becoming entirely too secular. I watch several church services online and on television and it amazes me that the congregation looks like they are coming to the club, the picnic or a sleep over; strapless dresses, cut off shorts, miniskirts, athletic gear, sagging pants, pajamas, head scarves, doo rags are just a few top fashions that I notice. I know we use God says come as you are as an excuse to go into the house of worship looking any kind of way but we need to stop for a minute and really think about our clothes and what they convey.

The way we dress has a lot to do with the way we think and where we are mentally. Think about it. When you go to play basketball, what do you wear? Why? If you are going for a job interview, what do you wear? Why? So if we do something a little extra to go to these places why don't we do a little extra when we come into the house to feast on the Word of the Lord. This is where we come to get encouragement and sustenance to help us make it one more week. Do you carry the same attitude that we talked about earlier…"God knows my heart"? Do you just give God anything? Do you make everything else your priority and God has to take what's left? Examine your life, where do you put your best foot forward?

When you are in Christ you are a new creature so why do you still look like the old creature? What you wear can dictate your mood and your thinking. When your pants are hanging down behind your knees, your hats to the back, and you have your gold fronts in, what kind of mood are you in? When I was partying all the time and living a fast life my closet reflected that. My tops were see through or low cut, my skirts were short, my jeans were tight, and all of my clothes looked happy (colorful and shiny). My clothes made me feel sexy so I acted sexy. I had a sexy walk, a sexy pout, a flirty come hither look, and sexy conversation. I was bad you couldn't tell me I wasn't dripping sex from head to toe. My clothes screamed for attention from the opposite sex. They said "hey I'm looking for a good time!" What are your clothes saying about you? Are your clothes hurting your witness?

We stereotype. I know that it's unfair and judgmental but it happens every day. You get or don't get a job based on a hiring manager's stereotype. People respond to you based on the way that you look. If you are neat, clean and well-groomed you get one response. If you are sloppy, clothes hanging off your body, smell and hair uncombed you get another response. They say it's important to always make a good first impression because first impressions are lasting impressions. When you walk into the door or into the room you make the first impression by the way that you look; before you ever open your mouth. When you open your mouth you can either confirm the impression or put a question mark over the impression. It's the same with witnessing to others. Their first impression and decision to hear what you have to say or not will be based on what you look like. You may have a great testimony and be very eloquent but you have to get their ear and attention first to be able to tell them your story. I know we think people are more open minded than that but they aren't.

I live in Atlanta where every time you exit the interstate, stop at a red light, or walk downtown someone is either asking you for money, trying to sell their CD, invite you to the club, ask you about being in a video, or giving you a sob story about a house that burned down with 10 other people and they were the only one that survived and now just need money so they can get out of the shelter that they're in. This makes you very wary of anyone walking up to you on the street and unfortunately it can also desensitize you to human suffering. That's why first impressions are very important because if you look like a bum on the street I'm going to think you're asking me for money so I may not take the time to listen to anything you're saying.

If your clothes are hanging off of you and you look unkempt, I'm going to think you're either trying to sell me something or rob me so once again I'm not taking the time to really listen to you. If all of your cleavage is on display and your skirt is barely covering your bottom I'm going to think that you're trying to ask me for some kind of help so once again I'm not taking the time to really listen to you. This may sound really ridiculous but this is how most people think especially this day and time.

You may take the stance that the way you dress shouldn't have anything to do with witnessing to people about Christ but unfortunately that is not the truth. It has a lot to do with how people will receive what you say or if they will believe you or not. It will also affect their desire to want to attend services at your church. Remember that first impression. Once they get to know you and see how you live how you dress will no longer matter. Your goal is to win them over to Christ so be careful to not let your first impression turn them away. This is also true for people who dress extremely dull. It's hard to attract people when you blend into the background or you look so pious and "holy" that any moment we're afraid you may be snatched to glory. That doesn't work either because you may seem unapproachable. I maintain that it may be very hard, particularly depending on where you live. Atlanta is very trendy. So much happens here that it's hard to find both men and women that aren't trying to make a fashion statement. I've visited churches that looked like Paris runway shows. Be wise.

[15] Be very careful, then, how you live—not as unwise but as wise

The above scripture, Ephesians 5:15 advises us to live carefully or the King James Version says to walk circumspectly. Circumspectly means watchful, vigilant, discreet, prudent and well considered. Let's look at that entire passage:

1. Follow God's example, therefore, as dearly loved children

2. and walk in the way of love, just as Christ loved us and gave himself up for us as a fragrant offering and sacrifice to God.

3. But among you there must not be even a hint of sexual immorality, or of any kind of impurity, or of greed, because these are improper for God's holy people.

4. Nor should there be obscenity, foolish talk or coarse joking, which are out of place, but rather thanksgiving.

5. For of this you can be sure: No immoral, impure or greedy person—such a person is an idolater—has any inheritance in the kingdom of Christ and of God.[a]

6. Let no one deceive you with empty words, for because of such things God's wrath comes on those who are disobedient.

7. Therefore do not be partners with them.

8. For you were once darkness, but now you are light in the Lord. Live as children of light

9. (for the fruit of the light consists in all goodness, righteousness and truth)

10. and find out what pleases the Lord.

11. Have nothing to do with the fruitless deeds of darkness, but rather expose them.

12. It is shameful even to mention what the disobedient do in secret.

13. But everything exposed by the light becomes visible—and everything that is illuminated becomes a light.

14. This is why it is said: "Wake up, sleeper, rise from the dead, and Christ will shine on you."

15. Be very careful, then, how you live—not as unwise but as wise,

¹⁶ making the most of every opportunity, because the days are evil.

¹⁷ Therefore do not be foolish, but understand what the Lord's will is.

¹⁸ Do not get drunk on wine, which leads to debauchery. Instead, be filled with the Spirit,

¹⁹ speaking to one another with psalms, hymns, and songs from the Spirit. Sing and make music from your heart to the Lord,

²⁰ always giving thanks to God the Father for everything, in the name of our Lord Jesus Christ.

²¹ Submit to one another out of reverence for Christ.

This is serious. Read this chapter and compare it with your day to day living, are you lining up with this word? Ultimately, light, the glory of God, is supposed to be reflected in us through our conversation, actions and attitude. Are you reflecting the Glory of God? Does your light shine or is it so dull that you blend in with everyone else, even unbelievers? Can you be picked out of a crowd as a son of God? The problem is that too many believers don't know how they are supposed to live and don't take their mission to witness seriously. There is no excuse. From Romans to Revelations the bible consistently tells us how to live the new life in Christ. There are even subtitles in chapters entitled, *The new life in Christ*. It is imperative that you understand your responsibility to others. When you receive salvation it is not a mission completed but a mission began. The goal is not for you only to be saved but for you to bring in others that are lost that need to be saved too. Your group of peers are your responsibility. You know how to relate to them, speak their language and empathize with their situations. You have the inside track to bringing them to Christ. The only way that you can lose your advantage is if you continue to do the same things that they do. They must see a new you; a change in conversation, actions and deeds. You can't play undercover cop and blend in to win them to Christ you have to show them something different and better.

In verse 15, Paul is telling us to be well considered. You may wonder how you can be well considered after you come to Christ if what you were doing before conversion was considered so low. Remember that you are a new creature. People that knew you before may not be able to ever accept that you have changed but remember the old things have passed away, behold all things have become new. It's up to you to walk in the new life in Christ. As you begin to walk therein, everyone will see a new you. Don't let your own shame and guilt stop you from witnessing to others. You are forgiven, Jesus' blood covers your sins so forgive yourself and get busy doing what you were created to do.

Let me reiterate that people that knew you before you accepted Christ may never accept that you are changed. Do not waste your time trying to convince them. Before I got really serious about living for Christ I drank a lot. I can remember that one year for my birthday the only gifts that I received were bottles of liquor. I celebrated by standing on a table with friends and being drenched with tequila that was being poured down my head and body before going to the club and partying until dawn. When I decided to change my life I went cold turkey. I stopped drinking immediately, and the smell of liquor, particularly rum and brandy, makes me extremely nauseous. None of my friends believed that I had quit drinking. Even after many years, when I am with my friends they offer me a drink or open a bar tab so I can have whatever I want. They will try to pressure me into drinking because they can't believe that I don't. It always amazes them when I order ginger ale. Don't get angry or discouraged when the people closest to you don't accept your change. Let their disbelief or amazement be a reminder of what God brought you out of and where He's brought you to and allow that to motivate you even more to share the Good News of Jesus Christ.

The best way to be successful at witnessing is to allow the Holy Spirit to lead you and guide you. He will teach you how to maintain your vessel and what to say. God will send many opportunities your way if it is your desire to witness.

God Has a Plan and Purpose for Our Lives

Many are the plans in a person's heart, but it is the Lord's purpose that prevails.   Proverbs 19:21

We've talked about God's plan and purpose for your life in almost every chapter. We must address it in this chapter also because this chapter is about the future and deciding who you want to be. It is important that you understand that who you want to be must line up with your purpose and work hand in hand with the plan that God has for your life. If not you will have a struggle or tug of war between who you want to be and who you were created to be. I think this happens to many famous people especially singers and musicians. Many R&B singers started in the church choir or singing gospel music. In time they switch over to secular music. They may toss in a gospel song or album but they are primarily known as secular artist; R & B, Pop, Soul, Country. I'm sure that the decision to sing secular music is for mass appeal and to make more money but I think that being a secular artist when your roots are in gospel is a conflict. It makes me think of a verse in Joshua 24:15, Choose you this day whom you will serve.

Why must we focus so much on plans and purpose?

Our lives should glorify God. Whatever we do should be done in the name of the Lord, giving thanks to God and it should be done heartily as unto the Lord and not unto men (Colossians 3:17, 23 paraphrased). Walking in our purpose and aligning our plans with that purpose allows others to see Christ in us and through us. Remember as Christians you are a part of the body of believers. If you don't operate in your purpose the body won't be effective and you won't live a whole, complete life.

Purpose is the reason for which anything is done, created, or exists. Remember you were created for a reason. Let me take some of the mystery out of this for you; your purpose doesn't have to be a huge undertaking; not everyone is called to pastor, prophesy, sing, run multimillion dollar companies, act, or do mission work in other countries. Your purpose could be to be a positive role model for boys and young men, you may not even realize the impact you can make. Just a word from you could save someone's life. You could be the teacher that challenges the student that one day finds a cure for AIDS. Only you can fulfill the purpose that God destined for you. You may be operating in your purpose right now but it may seem so insignificant to you that you miss it.

Think about screws; screws are used to hold things together. We use screws for almost everything: shelves, appliances, car parts, airplanes, beds, desks; this list can actually be exhaustive because almost everything that we use is held together by a screw. Screws come in many different shapes and sizes, they can be large and long or they can be really small and short, threaded or not, need a bolt or not. No one ever thinks about the screws when they look at an object and many times the screw is not seen but it plays a very important role because if it isn't seated well the object would shake or be unstable or if it isn't there the object would fall apart or not operate correctly. This is the same concept with your purpose. You may feel that your purpose is on the same level as the screw, seemingly insignificant, but despite the screws insignificance it has great impact: keeping things together and making things work.

> [28] And we know that in all things God works for the good of those who love him, who have been called according to his purpose. Romans 8:28

Knowing your purpose is knowing yourself. It also draws you closer to God because many of your questions are answered; what was once a mystery you can now see and understand. This awareness helps you to heal and make peace with your past experiences. If you know why you were created it's a lot easier to see why you had the life that you had. Remember Tyler Perry, look at all of the lives that he's touched. When you know who you are you are not easily deceived, derailed or destroyed. You understand yourself and where you fit in the body.

When I think of purpose, I always think of the movie *Lion King* and the circle of life. I can still recall James Earl Jones' deep voice as Mufasa, the father, explain the circle of life to his son, Simba. It was the simple fact that lions ate the antelope but when the lions died the nutrients in their bodies were absorbed into the earth and eventually got into the grass, which was then eaten by the antelope. Basically he was helping him to see how everything interconnects and how everything was created with purpose. The stages of the circle of life are the same stages of natural life: birth, growth, reproduction and death. These are also the stages of Christianity. You are born again, you grow in Christ, reproduce (be fruitful and multiply; purpose), and die. Just like naturally when you die your children (fruit) don't die, neither will the fruit from your purpose, it will bear more fruit from generation to generation for the edification of the whole body.

Remember everything that God created has purpose, you are no exception. Everyone's purpose is important no matter how great or small. Throughout the bible we meet men, women and even animals with purpose: Joseph saved Egypt and his family, God's chosen family throughout the famine. Daniel interpreted dreams and caused a whole nation to serve God; Rahab hid spies and helped the children of Israel be victorious; Esther spoke up to the king and saved the lives of the Jews; the donkey was available for Jesus to ride through the city to fulfill prophesy. These are just a few whose purpose seemed insignificant but made great impacts. Not to mention Abraham who was the Father of Many Nations, Mary who accepted the undertaking to be the mother of the Messiah; John the Baptist who preached in the wilderness, preparing the way and baptizing many; and let's not forget Noah. All mankind after the flood came through Noah's loins including the Messiah that came through his middle son Shem. Think about if Noah had not walked in his purpose. When God sent the flood everything with breath on the earth died except Noah, his family, and the animals that he took into the ark. When God had Noah take the animals into the ark his plan was to keep their seed alive. He had already put purpose in their seed. He could have killed all of the animals and even Noah and his family and start all over again but he chose not to. Why? Because they were created at that time for that purpose. The covenants that were made still stand to this day.

> 1. The Lord then said to Noah, "Go into the ark, you and your whole family, because I have found you righteous in this generation.
> 2. Take with you seven pairs of every kind of clean animal, a male and its mate, and one pair of every kind of unclean animal, a male and its mate,
> 3. and also seven pairs of every kind of bird, male and female, to keep their various kinds alive throughout the earth.
>
> (Genesis 7:1-3)
>
> 8. Then God said to Noah and to his sons with him:
> 9. "I now establish my covenant with you and with your descendants after you
> 10. and with every living creature that was with you—the birds, the livestock and all the wild animals, all those that came out of the ark with you—every living creature on earth.
> 11. I establish my covenant with you: Never again will all life be destroyed by the waters of a flood; never again will there be a flood to destroy the earth."
> 12. And God said, "This is the sign of the covenant I am making between me and you and every living creature with you, a covenant for all generations to come:
> 13. I have set my rainbow in the clouds, and it will be the sign of the covenant between me and the earth.
> 14. Whenever I bring clouds over the earth and the rainbow appears in the clouds,
> 15. I will remember my covenant between me and you and all living creatures of every kind. Never again will the waters become a flood to destroy all life.

> 16 Whenever the rainbow appears in the clouds, I will see it and remember the everlasting covenant between God and all living creatures of every kind on the earth."
>
> 17 So God said to Noah, "This is the sign of the covenant I have established between me and all life on the earth." (Genesis 9:8-17)

Wait I Say, On the Lord

> To everything there is a season, and a time to every purpose under the heaven.   Ecclesiastes 3:1

It is no coincidence that you are here right now, at this very moment, either in a class or sitting in your living room going through these pages. It is a part of your destiny and God has ordained it this way because now is the time to walk in your purpose.

As Ecclesiastes 3:1 says there is a time to every purpose under the heaven. Many times we look back over our lives and wish that we'd done some things sooner or waited to do some things, I know I've thought about some of the choices I made or projects that I undertook and wished I had done things differently. Even when you have a relationship with Christ you second guess your decisions and actions. I've learned to make peace with those things because I know if I am trying to walk in God's will for my life and ask Him to order my steps, He will. So I comfort myself with the fact that God orders my steps so I am where I'm supposed to be, when I'm supposed to be there. I had to get over feeling like I was behind, wasting time, or out of place or I wouldn't have accomplished anything.

It took me almost 14 years to finish my bachelor's degree. Can you imagine that, 14 years to finish a 4 year degree? I could have completed three 4 year degrees in 12 years and still have two years to spare. I started going to school when I was 18 years old, stationed in Shemya Alaska in 1988 and I finished my degree when I was 32 years old and stationed in Naples Italy in 2002. In those 14 years I got married, had a child, got divorced, single parented, got promoted several times, changed jobs several times, moved to Asia, moved to Europe, and got remarried. I was half way through a master's program when I received my diploma for my bachelor's degree. Ironically enough I completed a 2 year master's program in 1 year; I wasn't given my diploma until a year later but that's another story. I'm telling you this to let you know that timing is very important. We don't understand time the way that God does. His timing is not our timing.

I've learned that everything that I go through lines up with my purpose and the plan that God has for my life. I didn't understand that for many years so it made all of my challenges harder to deal with because I felt they were unnecessary. Sometimes things that should have been very easy and that worked out for everyone else completely collapsed for me. It made no logical sense…it worked for 100 people easily but as soon as it got to me it failed; the program had been suspended, money had dried up, policies had changed, company had shut down, cops had gotten involved; I would be utterly amazed. I had a hard time understanding this and would become frustrated and upset. When I would have a pity party about it, I would hear in my spirit, they that wait upon the Lord shall renew their strength, just wait. Wait…..

Waiting can be extremely challenging. Most of us hate waiting on anything. I know that I'm guilty of that. When I was in the military we had a saying "hurry up and wait". Being on time is a very important military discipline. Being late is not accepted and can get you into a lot of trouble. It was imperative that you be on time for everything; work, appointments, meetings, and even volunteering but no matter how early you'd arrive you would always have to wait. That's why the phrase was coined.

Waiting on God seems to be even more difficult than waiting for other things because we aren't always sure of when He will come or even how He will come. We may not even know what we're waiting for.

I've learned to wait on God the hard way. Whenever God showed me something I would do everything that I could to make it happen. Many times I would do the right thing but at the wrong time so I wouldn't get results; no fruit would come from it. When you pray and ask God for something He may answer some of those prayers immediately but some of them may not be answered for years. This is why it's important to ensure that when you pray you are lining up with God's word because God honors His word and will give you whatever you ask in Jesus' name. This knowledge helps you to wait patiently.

Waiting has several definitions; the definition that most people think of when they think of wait is "do nothing expecting something to happen: to stay in one place or do nothing for a period of time until something happens or in the expectation or hope that something will happen". That is not the type of waiting that I'm talking about because being in relationship with God requires action; doing nothing is not in line with the word of God. We must move, take action. Ecclesiastes 10:18 reminds us:

By much slothfulness the building decayeth; and through idleness of the hands the house droppeth through.

The definition of waiting that we will use is "be hoping for something: to be hoping for something or on the lookout for something". This is what our salvation is based on, hope. We are hoping for Jesus' return and our full redemption.

13   Therefore, with minds that are alert and fully sober, set your hope on the grace to be brought to you when Jesus Christ is revealed at his coming.

24   For in this hope we were saved. But hope that is seen is no hope at all. Who hopes for what they already have?

25   But if we hope for what we do not yet have, we wait for it patiently.

Romans 8:23-25

Patiently waiting is the challenge. We want everything now but being patient builds character. I won't pretend that it's easy but you get an opportunity to learn a lot about yourself while you're patiently waiting. Remember it's all about timing. I like the definitions of the word patient. Patient means able to endure waiting, delay, or provocation without becoming annoyed or upset; able to persevere calmly, especially when faced with difficulties; bearing pains or trials calmly or without complaint. I always like to say that I have patience but the truth is after seeing these definitions, I have a long way to go. The words that really get me are "without becoming annoyed or upset, calmly, and without complaint". While I may endure waiting and am able to persevere and bear pains or trials I may do it quietly or even with a smile on my face but many times I am annoyed, erratic and complaining. It is imperative that we learn to wait patiently because it will make our waiting easier. God is not going to move any faster if we are impatient because He knows the appointed time for everything that will occur in our lives. If we move too fast we may not be able to finish the race; if we move too slowly we may not be well equipped to go the distance. Once our waiting is over our strength will be renewed and we will be able to run on and see what the end is going to be.

The most important thing that I will encourage during your waiting is prayer. Have a dialogue with God; you speak and allow Him to speak to you. The more you pray and submit yourself you will become more accustomed to how the Holy Spirit lives, moves and speaks through you which will increase your sensitivity to his voice, his leading, and directing.

How do you move forward when you don't feel like you know your purpose? I think this is a problem for many Christians. I don't have a one size fits all answer there may be many reasons that you don't know your purpose or fill like God has shown you your purpose.

One of the reasons could be that you are still learning to listen and hear from God (remember Stop, Look and Listen), He may be telling you what your purpose is but you may not know His voice and may just dismiss it. You may be looking for something different. Remember the analogy about the screw? You may not be able to see your purpose as valuable. You may be rejecting your purpose. It may not be what you want to do, remember my daughter and the singing. You may be looking for something hard, new or challenging but many times your purpose lies in what comes naturally or easily to you. Remember you were created with your purpose so it has always been a part of you. Maybe you've lost sight of your purpose because you reinvent yourself too often. I think it's great to try new things and develop your mind and character but be careful not to do this all of the time because you may lose sight of who you are. Some people have so many things that they do well that they really don't perfect anything. Have you ever met anyone like that? They are so talented, creative, smart and innovative and can do so many things but end up doing absolutely nothing.

If you are struggling with knowing your purpose here is an exercise that may help you realize or identify your purpose. As I said, you may already be walking in your purpose and not realize it. Starting tomorrow, write down everything that you do from the moment that you get up to the moment that you go to bed. You don't have to put every single detail but some of the more relevant things like, what do you do on your way to work? Who did you talk to today, what did you talk about? What were your thoughts during and after the conversation? Do this for about a week. After a week is over look back at your entries to see if there are any correlations in different events. For example did you talk to several people about the same thing, on different days in different settings; did you console or offer advice to people; did you give to anyone several times in the week. These are just a few observations you can make but what I'm trying to get you to do is really pay attention to yourself and how you relate to others and your environment. Your purpose may be somewhere wrapped up in that. Also take time to really think about what you're good at, what you do effortlessly, what you really have passion for, many times that leads you to your purpose. If you're not sure ask others, whose opinions you trust and value, what they think your purpose is or where your strengths lie. My mother was able to help me identify my purpose. Of course you should do all of this in concert with praying and asking the Holy Spirit to lead and guide you into your purpose.

So maybe you're wondering how you can make plans if you don't know your purpose.

Let's talk about plans. The definition of plan is a scheme, program, or method worked out beforehand for the accomplishment of an objective. In the beginning we see God's plan unfold. When He created Adam, he gave him a plan. He was to "be fruitful and multiply, and replenish the earth and subdue it; and have dominion over the fish of the sea, and over the fowl of the air, and over every living thing that moveth upon the earth." (Genesis 1:28a)

Adam's fall caused God's plan for man to go awry. He could no longer be in fellowship as He'd planned with man because sin had entered the picture. Once sin was introduced into man's life he was separated from God. We begin to see God's plan for man quickly fall apart. We see God's ideal plan for marriage as Eve is brought to Adam and they are told to be fruitful and multiply, and to cleave together as one. As you continue to read through scripture you find out that the man is to love the woman as Christ loved the church, the woman is to reverence the man and the children are to obey the parents. What an ideal family that would be. Unfortunately finding that ideal family is like looking for a needle in a hay stack; especially in the United States.

Many times the way that we lived our lives before we accepted Christ had nothing to do with God's plan for us. We weren't really interested in what God's plan was. Many times we didn't even have a plan ourselves we were just winging it. Some of us still don't have a plan we are so overwhelmed with yesterday and today until there's no time to think about tomorrow. Matthew 6:34 tells us "Take therefore no thought for the morrow: for the morrow shall take thought for the things of itself. Sufficient unto the day is the evil thereof." Many Christians use this scripture to not prepare or make plans but that is not the intent. You must go back up to verse 24 that talks about serving two masters: God and mammon. Mammon is riches, so in essence this part of the Sermon on the Mount is talking about choosing between trusting God and trusting in your money or material possessions. So he's telling those that have wealth not to trust in wealth and those that don't have wealth not to worry about provision. Both of these situations will cause us to distrust God and not do His will. Verse 33 reminds us to seek first the kingdom of God and his righteousness because when we seek God first all of these material possessions will be given to us so that we won't have to think about what we will eat, drink or wear and can focus on God's plan and purpose for our lives.

To accomplish your purpose you must have a plan. You cannot accomplish your objectives if you don't have a plan. Think about it. You can't build a house without a plan, you wouldn't go to war without a plan, you wouldn't go on vacation to another country without a plan, you can't finish college without a plan, you can start a business without a business plan but you will not be able to get a loan, attract investors, or grow your business. You must even have a plan to walk in your purpose effectively. Plan's definition "a scheme, program, or method worked out beforehand; the accomplishment of an objective" means that before you can accomplish: achieve, fulfill or get results out of something you must take the time to plan: think about, arrange, formulate mentally, prepare, and strategize.

God is a planner, you can see this all throughout the Old Testament. Remember in Chapter 3, *What Does God Say About Me,* when we talked about the fall? God told them:

> "And I will put enmity between you and the woman, and between your offspring and hers; he will crush your head, and you will strike his heel."

If we were to count biblical time like we count time today (1 day is 24 hours) this scripture was written almost 4,000 years before the New Testament was written and Christ came to fulfill it. Imagine that, God worked out over 4,000 years beforehand how to accomplish his objective of redeeming mankind back to Himself. Because God is Omniscient we can assume that He'd made this plan many years before that because He knew the events that would happen in the Garden of Eden. Then throughout the Old Testament His plan begins to play out; we see Jesus foreshadowed and prophesy after prophesy foretells of His coming.

There are some plans that you must make just to exhibit a Christian lifestyle. We've talked about how you no longer live for yourself but for Christ. Changing doesn't just happen on its own you have to take steps to accomplish the objective of being changed, being transformed, being holy, submitting, and any of the other characteristics of a new creature. These things also work into your purpose because they will build your character. Your character plays a major role in walking in your purpose. You can't effectively walk in your purpose if your character is not developed.

Walking Purposefully

Many times when we become Christians we throw all practical and common sense out of the window; everything becomes spiritual. Whatever skills you have in the world can be used in the kingdom they just need to be used for the glory of God and for edification of the body. If you danced in the world you can dance in the kingdom, if you were a mover and shaker for the world, be a mover and shaker for the kingdom. Allow your whole self; your experiences, expertise, savviness, charisma and knowledge, to be expressed. God created us all individually, no two people are completely alike. We are not to try to be more like each other but more like Christ. It's important to know that because I listen to too many preachers trying to sound like and deliver a message like other preachers or too many singers trying to sing like other singers. You are unique; no carbon copy. What you deliver is different than what someone else delivers. Be who you were created to be and don't worry about being different because maybe you were not made to fit in but to stand out.

Be who God created you to be. If your purpose brings you to the foreground, come out of the shadow and work your purpose. If it puts you at the head of the line, hold your head up and lead the way. If it sits you in the director's chair, direct and control the flow. Do what you are supposed to do. Don't allow anyone to make you feel wrong for walking in your purpose. God knew what He was doing when He created and predestined you.

It won't be easy because when you begin to walk in your purpose, you will change. It may not be overnight but gradually as you begin to feel like you are doing what you were created to do you will feel fulfilled. You will get a bounce in your step, be more confident, and have a voice. You may not be able to explain it but everyone that knew you before will notice the change. There will be people that you love, are close to, and that are in your inner circle that will not be excited about this change. People that have been praying with you and for you will not be as excited as you thought they would be. People that were feeding you will no longer feel needed and people that were feeding on you will no longer feel comfortable and move on to someone else. Don't be surprised, don't let it get you down and don't let it stop you from moving forward in your purpose. Remember there's a time for everything.

The saying that people come into your life for a reason, a season, or a lifetime is very true. You just have to know the difference and be wise enough to let them go when it's time. Take it from me, when it's time to let go and move on just let go and move on. There have been times in my life when God said something was over; marriage, business relationship, relationships and friendships but I kept trying to stretch it out. Many times the people in these relationships were relying on or looking to me and I didn't know how to tell them that whatever we had was over. I was basically being disobedient. The Holy Spirit would speak to me about it, I would have dreams about it but I would keep making excuses to stay. None of the relationships were really fulfilling for me but I just didn't want to hurt the other party. Everything blew up in my face, each time. We'd get into a huge argument over nothing, the person would betray me, really strange stuff would happen and the other party had no problem ending the relationship immediately. It was like God was saying "I was trying to give you time to let go and move on but you didn't so I had to intervene." He had a purpose for me, he'd aligned events in my life for that purpose but I'd always allow myself to get distracted or derailed. Many times I wasn't doing anything wrong, normally I was helping others but I was out of the place He'd called me to.

Losing people can be painful because some people you thought would be in your life forever will leave. Just let them go, they served whatever purpose they were supposed to serve in your life. No matter what happens continue to walk in your purpose, continue to follow God's plan for your life and continue to trust God. All wounds heal; some take more time than others but if you live long enough they will heal.

I hate that we have to discuss the changes that will take place once you are walking in your purpose because it seems very negative but it is important that you are prepared. When you begin to seek after God and live righteously there will be a weaning process. People will begin to fall away, relationships will end and there will be times when you will feel all alone. You will have to believe and trust in the word of God like never before and encourage yourself. Not everyone that starts your journey will be with you at the end of your journey. I think this is the hardest part for Christians; the weaning process. Remember I said earlier that you can't play undercover cop when you're trying to bring others to Christ; there's no fitting in. If you continue to seek God and allow the Holy Spirit to lead and guide you, you will never be comfortable, not even in places where you used to wallow. You will be convicted quickly. You cannot try to live in purpose and live in the world too; you won't be effective.

… SHIFTING PARADIGMS FOR MEN

CHAPTER 9
Living Purposefully

We've talked extensively about plans and purpose now it's time to start planning purposefully. It is important to line up every area of your life with God's word. Some of the areas that we must focus on are:

- Daily Living
- Occupation
- Finances
- Health
- Relationships
- Service
- Witnessing

Below are areas that we will target to build a plan and create goals and objectives for; this is not all inclusive and may not apply to everyone. This is your plan you decide what areas you need to focus on.

Let's examine:

Daily Living – We talked about developing a Christian lifestyle. Read 1 Peter; 2 Corinthians 6:11-18; Romans 12:10-21; Romans 13:8-14. You must decide which elements need to be a part of your life and daily walk with Christ; areas that you may be weak in or are not walking in at all. Your plan should incorporate these vital traits/characteristics and actions of a new creature. Some examples are seeking God, loving one another, being trans- formed, being steadfast, exercising your faith.

Occupation – [17] And whatsoever ye do in word or deed, do all in the name of the Lord Jesus, giving thanks to God and the Father by him. [23]

And whatsoever ye do, do it heartily, as to the Lord, and not unto men; (Colossians 3:17, 23). God expects to get the glory out of every area of your life, even your work life. Examine your actions and attitude at work and make plans for God to get the glory.

Finances – Every man according as he purposeth in his heart, so let him give; not grudgingly, or of necessity: for God loveth a cheerful giver (2 Corinthians 9:7). Having the right frame of mind about finances are imperative. The bible tells us to give; not just tithes and offering but to give for the necessity of the saints. This lets us know that God expects us to be good stewards over what He has entrusted into our care, namely our finances. Examine your finances. Are you a giver? If not, why not? Are you in so much debt that you have nothing to give? If so, you need to make a plan to improve your finances so that you can be in line with the word. If you spend too much and don't have enough to give you need to make a plan to control your spending. Only you know your financial picture and what needs to happen so that you can be a good steward and able to advance the kingdom.

Health – [2] Dear friend, I pray that you may enjoy good health and that all may go well with you, even as your soul is getting along well (3 John 1:2). You cannot be effective in the kingdom if you are not in good health. Healthy mind, body and soul. It's important that you take care of your body which is the temple of the Holy Ghost; God dwells within you. You need to be careful of what you allow in your mind, in your body, and what gets into your soul. What areas do you need to work on? If you need to get in shape physically, make a plan for better eating and exercising; if you need your thinking to change, Philippians 4:8 tells us what to think on: Finally, brothers and sisters, whatever is true, whatever is noble, whatever is right, whatever is pure, whatever is lovely, whatever is admirable—if anything is excellent or praiseworthy—think about such things. [19] In your patience possess ye your souls **Luke 21:19.**You are in control of what and who is in your life and their affects upon your character and lifestyle.

Relationships – Examine all of your relationships and ensure that they are lining up with God's word. I will give just a few scriptures because there are so many: **Ephesians 6:1-3** [1] Children, obey your parents in the Lord, for this is right. [2] "Honor your father and mother"— which is the first commandment with a promise— [3] "so that it may go well with you and that you may enjoy long life on the earth." **Colossians 3:18** - Wives, submit yourselves to your husbands, as is fitting in the Lord. Read Colossians 3:12-24 for how to treat other believers. Go through and find other scriptures that deal with relationships. Make your plan to target areas where your relationships are not lining up.

Service – We are one body and are supposed to love and serve one another. - [1] Therefore if you have any encouragement from being united with Christ, if any comfort from his love, if any common sharing in the Spirit, if any tenderness and compassion, [2] then make my joy complete by being like-minded, having the same love, being one in spirit and of one mind. [3] Do nothing out of selfish ambition or vain conceit. Rather, in humility value others above yourselves, [4] not looking to your own interests but each of you to the interests of the others **Philippians 2:1-4**. Where are you falling short?

Witnessing – We've talked about the Great Commission extensively and that you are to be a witness. God's kingdom will only advance if we tell others about the goodness of the Lord. Make a plan to incorporate witnessing into every day of your life.

There are many tools that you can use in planning to help set objectives and meet goals so feel free to use whatever tool you like. I created a tool from the words PRAISE because all that you do should be a praise unto God.

PRAISE stands for Purpose, Realistic, Analyze, Intentional, Specific, Executable, and you can add Re-evaluate for PRAISER.

Letter	Most Common	Alternative
P	Purpose	Preparation
R	Realistic	Rational
A	Analyze	Anticipate
I	Intentional	Interesting
S	Supernatural	Simple
E	Executable	Evaluate
R	Reevaluate	Routine

Purpose

Ensure that your goals and objectives line up with your purpose and preparation. Every trial or tribulation has been for some reason and many times that reason is to prepare you for what is to come while walking in your purpose. Ask yourself questions like: Am I sure of my purpose? In what ways have I been preparing for my purpose?

Realistic

You must ensure that the goals that you set for yourself are "doable" for you and can meet your purpose. Ask yourself questions like: Will I really commit myself to this goal and the objectives that I've set? How does this goal meet my purpose? Are my motives right? Am I going about it the right way? Did I seek God about it?

Analyze

Once you realize that the goal aligns with your purpose ensure that you look at different ways to meet the goal, the outcome and what challenges or obstacles may stand in your way. Ask yourself questions like: Can I realistically meet the goal? Do I have everything that I need to meet the goal? What are possible obstacles that may hinder me reaching the goal? Can I eliminate the obstacles? If so, how?

Intentional

Be intentional about what you are doing to ensure that you can get the outcome that you desire. Make sure that every step that you put in place works toward your desired outcome. Keep it interesting! Planning is an opportunity to make your life better; more fruitful and more productive. Try new things, challenge yourself and make the goals enjoyable. Ask yourself questions like: Will my objectives work again and again? Will what I've put in place, help me meet my goals? Am I enjoying myself?

Supernatural

Remember that you do not have to do this alone…you have supernatural help. Allow God to be a part of your planning. Being led by the Holy Spirit, reading the word of God and allowing God to order your steps will help you succeed. Ask yourself questions like: Have I prayed about my goals? Do I believe that God is happy with my goals? Do I need other support?

Executable

Evaluate the plan to ensure that it's doable and then Execute! Execute! Execute! After you've taken time to make the goals, execute your plans to meet them. Don't waste time working on a plan that you never put into action. If you are faithful to execute, God will help you excel. Ask yourself questions like: Do the steps that I've put in place work? When do I start working the plan? How much time can I dedicate to the plan? Does the plan fit into my current lifestyle? If not, what changes do I need to make? Am I willing to make the changes?

Re-evaluate

After executing your plan you may find that there are changes that you can make, make them and continue on. It's important that you re-evaluate along the way to make things easier and better for yourself. Once it's working for you make it a part of your routine so that you create healthy habits. Ask yourself questions like: What worked best?

What didn't work? What can I change? How did my plan impact others? Can I do better?

This is a personal thing and should be undertaken after sitting down, examining each of the focus areas that we've discussed (Daily Living, Occupation, Finances, Health, Relationships, Service, and Witnessing) and determining where you need improvement or where you need a jump start. We will help you get started in class because hearing others' goals and objectives can help you create your own.

Let's start by writing down a goal for each of our focus areas. Use a separate PRAISE worksheet for each goal. Fill in the PRAISE information, it doesn't have to be perfect, it can change, as a matter of fact it may change. This exercise will just help you get started.

Goal for Daily Living:

P_____	
R_____	
A_____	
I_____	
S_____	
E_____	

Goal for Occupation:

P_____	
R_____	
A_____	
I_____	
S_____	
E_____	

Goal for Finances:

P_____	
R_____	
A_____	
I_____	
S_____	
E_____	

Goal for Health:

P_____	
R_____	
A_____	
I_____	
S_____	
E_____	

Goal for Relationships:

P_____	
R_____	
A_____	
I_____	
S_____	
E_____	

Goal for Services:

P_____	
R_____	
A_____	
I_____	
S_____	
E_____	

Other Goal _____

P_____	
R_____	
A_____	
I_____	
S_____	
E_____	

CHAPTER 10

Sustaining The Shift

So Now What? This is actually the name of a book series that God gave me years ago maybe I will write it to help you continue your journey of paradigm shifting. Be looking for it.

These training sessions have given you lots of food for thought and hopefully if you were honest enough with yourself and really got involved in each session you were able to make changes in your life and begin to shift your paradigm. Shifting paradigms is not easy because many of our thoughts and beliefs have been ingrained in us for many years. I know that you're thinking "it will take more than one training series to completely change my life" and you may be right but it's not impossible. As we've discovered over and over throughout the sessions, it's all about the way that you think. As a man thinketh in his heart so is he. Shifting paradigms is about **you** changing **your** thinking about **yourself**, **your life**, **your experiences**, **your relationships** and **your future**. Nothing will ever change in your life if you don't change the way that you think about it. If you want a positive outcome but only think negatively you will not get positive. If you think you can never do any better, guess what, you won't.

My goal has been to challenge your thinking about everything; your past, your relationship with God, your relationship with others, your Christian lifestyle and your purpose. When Christ told the disciples that He would send the Holy Spirit, in John 16:13 He called Him the Spirit of truth, He would guide them into **all** truth. Not just some truth, not just truth about Christ and His work on the cross but **all** truth.

> ¹³ Howbeit when he, the Spirit of truth, is come, he will guide you into all truth: for he shall not speak of himself; but whatsoever he shall hear, that shall he speak: and he will shew you things to come. John 16:

So what does that mean for you? We have been examining the truth throughout the sessions and this truth is what has brought about a shift in your paradigm. When you know the truth you can no longer be bound because the truth brings about change; makes us free to choose, to love, and to grow. Think about it. When you know all of the details of a situation you can more readily deal with that situation or even choose not to deal with it. Christ told His disciples that He is the way, **the truth**, and the life. So when we open our minds and spirits to the truth and walk therein we are being transformed into the image of Christ.

When God allowed His glory to pass by Moses although Moses was hidden in the cleft of the rocks and covered with God's hand just seeing the backside of God caused Moses' countenance to change; his face shone. Moses had to put a veil over his face because he had to hide the truth from the Israelites because they were not able to handle it. When Christ died on the cross the veil was rent or torn which allowed us access to God and ultimately access to the truth.

> ¹² Therefore, since we have such a hope, we are very bold.
>
> ¹³ We are not like Moses, who would put a veil over his face to prevent the Israelites from seeing the end of what was passing away.
>
> ¹⁴ But their minds were made dull, for to this day the same veil remains when the old covenant is read. It has not been

> removed, because only in Christ is it taken away.
>
> ¹⁵ Even to this day when Moses is read, a veil covers their hearts.
>
> ¹⁶ But whenever anyone turns to the Lord, the veil is taken away.
>
> ¹⁷ Now the Lord is the Spirit, and where the Spirit of the Lord is, there is freedom.
>
> ¹⁸ And we all, who with unveiled faces contemplate the Lord's glory, are being transformed into his image with ever-increasing glory, which comes from the Lord, who is the Spirit.
>
> 2 Corinthians 3:12-18

How do you apply this to your life? By reading the Word of God and by allowing the Holy Spirit to guide you. The Holy Spirit illuminates the word and also bears witness with our spirit because He convinces us of the truth that can only be understood through divine help. He gives us unveiled vision. As you allow the Holy Spirit to have more of you He will tell you what He hears from God concerning you. This makes it hard to be deceived about who you are, what your purpose is and what lies in your future because you will be armed with the truth.

Don't confuse this desire for truth with some of the teachings of other sects, religions or groups that are seeking knowledge, light and self-actualization. God is your source for all things. You don't have to seek light because you are light and there's no such thing as self-actualization in the kingdom. Be careful not to be led astray by those who are on a quest for truth apart from God's word.

2 Timothy 3:1-9 puts it best:

¹ But mark this: There will be terrible times in the last days.

² People will be lovers of themselves, lovers of money, boastful, proud, abusive, disobedient to their parents, ungrateful, unholy,

³ without love, unforgiving, slanderous, without self-control, brutal, not lovers of the good,

⁴ treacherous, rash, conceited, lovers of pleasure rather than lovers of God—

⁵ having a form of godliness but denying its power. Have nothing to do with such people.

⁶ They are the kind who worm their way into homes and gain control over gullible women, who are loaded down with sins and are swayed by all kinds of evil desires,

⁷ always learning but never able to come to a knowledge of the truth.

⁸ Just as Jannes and Jambres opposed Moses, so also these teachers oppose the truth. They are men of depraved minds, who, as far as the faith is concerned, are rejected.

⁹ But they will not get very far because, as in the case of those men, their folly will be clear to everyone.

The devil, your adversary, as a roaring lion walks around seeking whom he may devour. Think back to the last person that tried to hurt you or destroy you, what did they use? Normally a lie or some form of deceit. That's why it's so important that you know the truth. Even when you are in Christ if you are not armed with the truth you can be easily persuaded, be double minded, tossed to and fro and although you have eternal life you are having eternal hell breaking out in your life all of the time.

This is not the life predestined for you. God wants you to have peace that surpasses all understanding and He wants you to live victoriously. You already have the victory why not express that in every area of your life. Completing this course is not a mission accomplished but a mission began. Hopefully these sessions were building blocks to help you strengthen your foundation in preparation for growth. Stay focused on purposefully planning until it becomes a part of your everyday walk. My prayer for you is that you prosper, even as your soul prospers.

Prayer:

Father I thank you for this student of life. I ask that you bless him to continue to grow in faith and increase his desire for truth. Give him a mind to walk in the newness of life and to lean not unto his own understanding but in all of his ways to acknowledge you and let you direct his path. I stand against the enemy and his tactics to try to snatch every morsel that he has feasted on. I ask that you let every word that was spoken be a life changing word for him and that he is steadfast, unmovable and always abounding in your word and in your work. Bless his home and family. Build up every torn down area and break every stronghold. I stand in agreement with him now. In the mighty and precious name of Jesus, I pray. Amen

High five someone and declare "My paradigm has been shifted".

NOTES/REFERENCES

[1] http://changingminds.org/explanations/behaviors/coping/coping.htm

[2] http://www.tylerperry.com/biography/

[3] http://www.brainyquote.com/quotes/authors/t/tyler_perry.html#qBpd5EdwQJmERywt.99)

[4] http://www.notable-quotes.com/w/williams_fannie_barrier.html

[5] http://martinlutherkingjrquotes.org

[6] Scofield's Reference Notes http://www.studylight.org/com/srn/ view. cgi?book=ge&chapter=017)

[7] http://www.gotquestions.org/image-ofGod .html#ixzz2meRNsNwB

[8] http://www.lionlamb.us/lion/lionfact.html

[9] http://www.ronedmondson.com/2009/12/10-reasons-david-is-a-man- after-god%E2%80%99s-own-heart.html

[10] https://www.christiancourier.com/articles/1385-some-character- traits-of-paul-the-apostle

[11] www.biblestudy.org

[12] www.bartleby.com (The Creation by James Weldon Johnson)

All Scriptures are from New International Version (NIV) Holy Bible, New International Version®, NIV® Copyright © 1973, 1978, 1984, 2011 by Biblica, Inc.® unless otherwise noted.

www.ingramcontent.com/pod-product-compliance
Lightning Source LLC
Chambersburg PA
CBHW050538300426
44113CB00012B/2164